PAINLESS SEWING

With Pretty Pati's Perfect Pattern Primer

And Ample Annie's Awful but Adequate Artwork

By Pati Palmer and Susan Pletsch

A special thank you to Palmer/Pletsch associates who taught time-saving techniques through the years, especially Lynn Raasch, Marta Also, Leslie Wood, and Lynette Black. Also a thank you to our husbands Dave Bosworth and Jack Watson and Pati's daughter, Melissa. A final thank you to editor par excellence, Ann Price Gosch. How can she be so young and know so much about grammar!

**Cartoonist
Jo Reid**

Library of Congress Catalog Card No. 86-090509

Published by Palmer/Pletsch, Inc., www.palmerpletsch.com
1801 NW Upshur Street, Suite 100,Portland, Oregon 97209

Revised design and production by Wisner Creative, Portland, Oregon
Illustrations by the authors, Kate Pryka, and Patty West

Fourth Edition ISBN-13: 978-0-935278-54-5

Pati Palmer

Susan Pletsch

About the Authors

Pati Palmer and Susan Pletsch have developed careers promoting a favorite hobby, sewing. They have co-authored four sewing books, established a publishing company that has produced dozens of books and videos, and traveled across North America teaching seminars. They have designed for Vogue Pattern Company and then for McCall's from 1980 to present.

Pati and Susan met as educational representatives for Armo, a shaping fabrics manufacturer. Pati has also been corporate home economist for an Oregon department store, as well as buyer of sewing notions. Pati graduated from Oregon State University in home economics. She served as national chairman of the Business Section of the American Association of Family and Consumer Sciences and was selected Oregon Home Economist of the Year. She has been vice-chairman of education for the American Home Sewing and Craft Association and served as a trustee on the Oregon 4-H Foundation board.

Susan has been a home economist with Talon Consumer Education, where she traveled extensively giving consumer and educator workshops. She graduated from Arizona State University and taught home economics to special education students. Susan "retired" from the business several years ago to marry and travel with her husband. She still sews for herself and home and writes articles for national publications.

... and their friends ...

Ample Annie is Anne Peterson who left an "8 to 5" job to begin her own custom uniform factory (located in her second bedroom!). Her first contract was for 150 band uniforms, which she designed and sewed herself in less than four weeks. Imagine this — making 1200 buttonholes — sewing on 1200 buttons — **and** setting in 300 sleeves. Annie is our resident expert in daredevil speed.

Speedy but elegant describes the sewing methods used by Marta McCoy Alto, past costume mistress and super-custom seamstress who now teaches seminars for Palmer/Pletsch Associates. Marta sews faster and yet better than anyone else we know. She has the magic touch in turning fabric into a couture garment overnight.

Ample Annie's sister Jo Reid is actually our inspired cartoonist. Annie had the idea — but Jo has the touch. Jo, an art education graduate from Oregon College of Education, was once a sewing "dropout," but has since reconsidered and is giving it another chance.

Table of Contents

But I don't have the patience to sew...

Mother Pletsch's Painless Sewing will not try to convince you that you should sew—that's your decision. But for all of the rest of us who are hooked on sewing, there is hope. **There is an easier way!**

We learned to sew in the same ways as many of you — on our own, from our mother, or home economics teachers — and our teachers were possibly no better or worse than yours. So why are we loving our hobby and profession of sewing while you curse the same?

Seventy (yes 70!) years of combined experience helps. (We started to sew as very small children!!) But the real answers are attitudes, believing in the power of positive thinking, and insisting on finding the easier way. We are incurable optimists. We will always look at a half glass of water and say it is half full. The power of positive thinking lives in sewing too. If you think the dress is going to be gorgeous — it will be! Or we will help you find a way to make it gorgeous.

We feel that sewing is such a personal and an individual thing that there simply cannot be a "right" way to complete a given task. We find that even we often disagree on the easiest or best way because we are two different people. So, whenever necessary, we will illustrate more than one way. Be flexible and try them all. Remember that finding a method that's easy for you is somewhat like buying new shoes. Unless you try on every possible pair, you will never know if you bought the most comfortable ones.

Sewing should be quick, but we also believe in making something that looks good enough to wear. No more half-finished things donated to your favorite charity clothing drive. (They don't sell there either!) Fashionable, attractive, perfect-fitting garments are the desirable end product. With a bit of experience, you too will be able to make a linen blazer in eight hours like Pati, or a gorgeous blouse in two hours like Susan. So here it is...everything you wanted to know about sewing, but were afraid to ask — hassle-free sewing, sinfully simple sewing, and all those little tricks and tips and hints and shortcuts that can save your sanity and make sewing **FUN, FAST, AND EASY... AND PAINLESS!!!**

How to Sew Fast!

Speedy sewing is an art. Like singing ability, some people naturally have it and some don't. But also like singing, it is possible for us to discipline ourselves to do better. Study "How to Sew Fast" and force yourself to follow our suggestions for **one month** and see if you can't improve your sewing speed.

Ready, set, ... sew!!!

The daredevil seamstress speaks: Ample Annie says, "In order to sew fast . . . . ."

1. Turn off all music, TV, and radio noise while cutting out a pattern — that is when you need to concentrate.

2. Turn on speedy banjo or intense Beethoven music when sewing.

3. Take the telephone off the hook until you are ready to do handwork.

4. Eat or drink energy food.

How to Sew Fast: Ten Tips

1. **Cut your fabric with right sides together** so all center front and center back seams are in a ready-to-sew position. **AND — use your hands for pins!** Pin only the corners of the pattern. Cut, holding the pattern flat with one hand. Or, use a rotary cutter — great for trimming around patterns.

2. **Snips - not notches.** When cutting, keep marking and pinning to a minimum by using a ¼" snip into the seam allowance to indicate a notch. We have often been told not to clip into a seam allowance because we may need to let out the seam, but if you need to get into that last ¼", you are in deep trouble anyway. So...**snip-mark** center front, center back, notches, top of sleeves, hem folds, and other "joining" points.

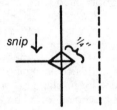
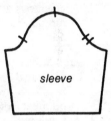

sleeve

3. **Put your foot on the accelerator** and **force** your machine to sew fast. It does take somewhat slower stitching to do smooth curves, but learn to sew as fast as your machine will stitch on all straight seams, in staystitching, and in seam finishing. Sewing fast will not hurt your machine!

4. **Continuous sewing.** It takes time and thread to stop at the end of each seam, clip threads and start over. Instead, stitch immediately from one seam to another. Use continuous sewing when:

   1. Staystitching
   2. Sewing seams*
   3. Finishing seams

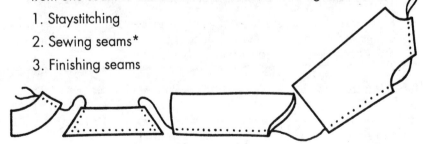

*You may still backstitch where you normally would when continuous sewing.

5. **Consolidated sewing** — "Press as you sew" is a super idea, but we would all have wrestler's thighs from getting up each time we needed to press one seam. Save time and your thigh muscles by sewing as many seams as possible before going to the iron. Stop sewing only when you have to cross another seam that should be pressed open first.

Do as much as possible at one time and divide sewing into FOUR BLOCKS OF TIME:

1. **Planning and Fitting (25% of total sewing time)** – In this block you fit your pattern and collect everything you'll need to sew this garment. STOP!

2. **Cutting, Marking, Applying Interfacing, and Pinning Pieces into a Ready-to-Sew Position** – Don't stop after cutting. It's much easier to apply interfacing while all the pieces are flat. Then pin all you can sew together. STOP!! Next time you sew, it will be easy. Even at 5 a.m. we can sew a seam. No thinking is required.

3. **Sew and Press** – This could be more than one session. The point here is to **prepare** for finishing as well. Have you ever sewn a garment that is still waiting for a hem? Before the "sewing" segment is finished, pin up the hem, gather hooks or buttons, thread, needle, scissors and pin cushion, and put them in a plastic bag and attach to the hanger. Now quit!

4. **Finishing** – Now you are ready for TV or telephone work! Take finishing work along on a trip or to visit with friends.

Consolidated sewing also means that it is easier to make two shirts at the same time, especially if you use the same pattern. If one shirt can be made in 2 hours, two shirts can be made in 3 hours.

6. **Flat First!** This means to complete flat pieces before joining side seams. It's not easy to sew in a tube. For example, sew collar to a dress neckline before sewing the side seams.

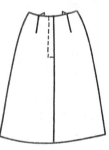

Insert zipper and sew darts before sewing side seams.

Put on pockets before joining front to back.

7. **Jam-proof sewing** means holding onto the upper thread for the first 3-4 stitches in a seam. This prevents jammed threads, which take time to unjam, and also saves frustration.

8. **Taut sewing** — a super technique that allows any number of layers and weight of fabrics to feed evenly through the machine with no machine adjustments. Pull equally on your fabric in font of and behind the needle as you sew. Do not stretch, just pull until "taut" as if you were sewing with your fabric in an embroidery hoop. However, let the fabric feed through the machine on its own.

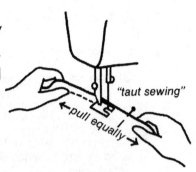

"taut sewing"

pull equally

NOTE: Taut sewing is automatic pucker prevention on most fabrics. Use it when sewing polyester woven fabrics, Ultrasuede®, permanent-press fabrics, velvet, and microfiber fabrics.

9. **Tie threads?? No No!!** Try one of the following methods instead:

- Knot in place by lifting the presser foot ⅛" and holding onto the fabric with a finger on each side of the presser foot so the fabric won't move, and stitch in place three or four times.

- Turn your machine to "0" stitch length, stitch three or four times in place.

- Drop feed dogs to stitch three or four times in place.

- Backstitch, but at seam intersection, not at the edge that will be trimmed away. Your seams will be **much** stronger.

- Use the automatic lockstitch feature found on many computerized machines.

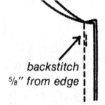

backstitch
⅝" from edge

10. **The obvious — know your machine.** Learn to use it to the fullest. If you don't know how to use the buttonholer, for example, sit down at the machine for 30 minutes making nonstop buttonholes in a scrap of fabric. We guarantee that you'll learn to make excellent machine buttonholes if you do this. PRACTICE using your accessories!

Now that we have given you a few tips on how to sew faster, we are going to talk about a "concept" of sewing that is much more important than any single tip — organization!

1. **Organization** in sewing habits (see tips 1 through 10).
2. **Organization** of your sewing room and tools.
3. **Organization** of shopping and wardrobe planning.

Room and Tools

Ideally, a sewing room, closet, or corner should have the following:

1. Mug rack on the wall.
2. Full-length mirror.
3. Chest of drawers next to the machine for small supplies and storing fabric and notions — and for your own personal interfacing "store."
4. Surface that can be used for both cutting and pressing and that can remain set up at all times. (See Cut 'n' Press board, page 28.)
5. Waste basket or paper bag attached to machine.
6. Bulletin board (nice if above the machine to hold guide sheets).
7. Table that holds *both* sewing machine and serger—or two tables.

It's like trying to sew efficiently in a football field!

Being able to close a door or put up a screen to hide the sewing area is **MUST!** Leaving your projects out as sewing is in progress is more that a luxury — it is the way to **sanity**. The amount of space you have is not really important; organization of that space is the real key. We know a woman who has a huge basement for a sewing room. It's like sewing in a football field. It takes her forever to complete one garment because things are so far apart. She has **too much room**.

Shopping and Wardrobe Planning

— a crazy way to sew fast, but they really are related.

Do you have a closet full of clothes and nothing to wear? What a tragic waste of all the time spent sewing that closet-full. Wouldn't it be better to have spent half the time making half the clothes and yet still have **twice** as much to wear?

Coordinate and Consolidate

- Don't be a pack rat. Get rid of what you don't wear, then you won't feel guilty about making new things.
- Planning makes the most of the sewing time you **do** have. When you coordinate, one blouse can go with four outfits, and you don't have to make four different blouses.
- Pick one or two **base** colors and plan around these. They don't have to be basic blue or brown. Choose magenta or tangerine if that thrills you!
- Don't be a remnant queen. Buy six yards of a good solid-colored fabric that you love and make pants, skirt, and jacket. Then accessorize and mix and match. It saves $$$, shopping time and **sewing time**.

- Carry color swatches with you! Buy one of those plastic accordion-fold wallet-photo holders for swatches and favorite pattern yardage requirements. Look at it every time you make a fabric or accessory purchase and slap your hand if your new purchase doesn't fit into the "grand scheme of things."

- Having a good color analysis to learn your best colors will save you time and money by reducing impulse buying and eliminating poor color choices. Color knowledge helps you find new combinations of items already in your closet, and wearing your best colors helps you feel good about your appearance.

Smart Shopping Saves Time, Money, and Hassle

1. Solid colors are more versatile and faster to sew than plaids. **For speed** avoid plaids — they look great but require cutting and matching skill and concentration. Prints that do not require matching are fast to sew because they hide all kinds of mistakes and make a very simple pattern look great. Wool and wool-blend tweeds are the fastest fabrics to sew because they hide mistakes and press and shape easily.

2. Buy the best quality fabric you can afford. It will be easier to sew and will reward you by looking like a million dollars for years. Besides, you're going to have fewer items to wear, so what you have must be more durable.

3. Buying patterns takes time — make every pattern at least twice to save looking time and sewing time **plus $$$**. Different fabrics change the whole look of a pattern anyway.

4. If you're going to copy ready-to-wear, copy the best! Go to the custom or designer shops to snoop-shop. Try it on and see if it's you. Don't copy bargain basement ideas. It's a waste of your precious time and talent.

5. Don't waste time making something you can afford to buy unless you can't get a good fit or the right color.

From Fiber to Fabric

If you feel you already have a good understanding of the selection and care of all the fibers and fabrics that are on the market, don't bother reading this chapter — that wouldn't be painless sewing. But if you are unsure . . .

FIBERS — fibers are fine hair-like substances that are used in making yarns that are woven or knitted into fabrics.

Generic names — a name of a "family" of fibers similar in composition such as polyester or nylon.

Brand names — first names given to fibers by the chemical companies that make them. For example, DuPont® named one of its polyester fibers Dacron®.

How Fibers and Yarns Are Made

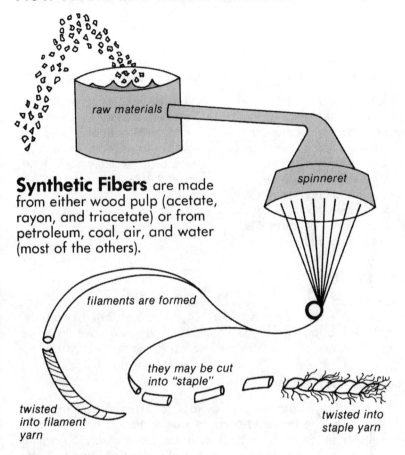

raw materials

spinneret

Synthetic Fibers are made from either wood pulp (acetate, rayon, and triacetate) or from petroleum, coal, air, and water (most of the others).

filaments are formed

they may be cut into "staple"

twisted into filament yarn

twisted into staple yarn

Natural Fibers are either protein-based or cellulose-based. The fibers are twisted together to form yarns. Silk fibers are the longest and silk yarn is the shiniest and smoothest. Wool fibers are very short. Wool yarn is the fuzziest.
Protein fibers — silk (unwound from the silkworm's cocoon) and wool (short fibers from the fleece of a sheep)
Cellulose fibers — linen (from the stems of the flax plant) and cotton (made from the seed pod of the cotton plant)

Blended Fabrics are made of yarns that are composed of two or more fibers to improve the appearance of the fabric, improve the fabric performance or comfort, make the fabric easier to produce, or make expensive fibers go further by combining them with less expensive ones. Blends provide the best of both worlds! Spandex (Lycra®) is blended with cotton or wool to improve resiliency.

What Does the Length of a Fiber Do for a Fabric?

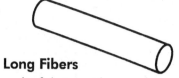

Long Fibers

make fabrics with smoother surfaces that often wear better. If **synthetic**, the fabrics are often stronger. If natural, longer fibers make the best quality fabrics. They wrinkle less, are more resilient, and pill less. This is why wool gabardine wears better than a wool flannel — because it is made from longer fibers.

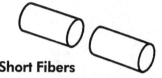

Short Fibers

If **synthetic**, they are called "staple," and are cut short to imitate natural fibers. Have you noticed how Orlon® acrylic sweaters look like wool? They are soft, lofty, and fuzzy.

Fiber Width

Microfibers are in the news! They are so fine that a mere pound can circle the earth at the equator (24,901.55 miles)! Ultrasuede® was the first fabric to be made from microfibers. We love the sand-washed rayon and polyester microfiber fabrics we see today.

Fiber Absorbency

The moisture absorbency of a fiber is an important factor in wear and care. The **more absorbent fibers** are more comfortable to wear, because they pick up body moisture and humidity. Since they absorb moisture, they are less prone to static electricity and will also clean more easily. The **less absorbent fibers** are less comfortable to wear, but since they are less affected by body heat and moisture, they wrinkle less and hold their shape better. They are more prone to static electricity so can pill more readily.

Use the following **absorbency scale** as a guide in fabric selection.

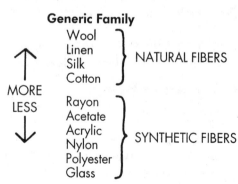

Rayon, the most absorbent synthetic, is actually as absorbent as most of the natural fibers, but the other synthetics are all much less absorbent.

NOTE: Remember that this scale is true 90% of the cases today, but if more altering is done to fibers or if finishes are applied, it will be less true.

Fiber Modification

Why do some synthetics differ from others made from the same ingredients? It's because of "fiber modification." This means changing basic synthetic fibers by simply changing the shape of the holes from which the fibers are extruded (pushed out) in the manufacturing process. Dacron VIII polyester has an octalobal cross-section because it is extruded from an eight-sided hole.

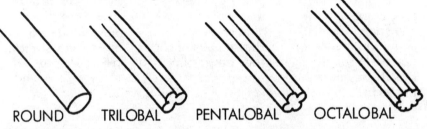

ROUND   TRILOBAL   PENTALOBAL   OCTALOBAL

Modification may change the characteristics of the fabric by making it . . . . .
1. Less clingy and static prone
2. More resistant to soil
3. Breathe better (more channels for moisture)
4. Deeper, richer color
5. Less shiny

Texturizing for Stretch

Texturizing a synthetic filament yarn causes a coil or crimp that provides a stretch characteristic to a woven or knitted fabric. It also makes fabrics lighter weight and loftier.

This kind of texturizing can be done only to thermoplastic synthetic fibers such as nylon and polyester, because they have the ability to be softened and shaped or "heat set." It cannot be done to those made from wood pulp.

A texturized yarn:

Fabric

The fibers and yarns we have been discussing can be made into a number of different fabrics.

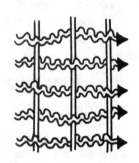

Nonwovens
Made by bonding fibers together. They don't ravel. Some stretch, some don't and some stretch only in one direction.

Wovens
Made by inter-weaving yarns at right angles. They don't stretch. They do ravel.

Stretch-Wovens
Made with textur-ized yarns. They may be one-way or two-way stretch. They do ravel.

Loops vs. Lines — Yarns in wovens run in straight lines across the fabric, but knits are a series of interlocking loops. Knits stretch and don't ravel.

Single Knits — Made with a single needle. They stretch in both directions, have lengthwise "wales" on the right side and crosswise "courses" on the wrong side, and roll to the right side when stretched on the cross grain. Sweater knits and jersey are popular varieties.

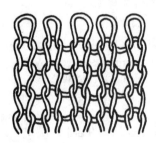

Double-Knits — Made with two sets of needles. Plain ones look the same on both sides. There are many varieties including inter-locks.

So What is the Big Textile Deal!

How does all this information help you? First decide what qualities are important for you to be happy with the finished product. For example, does a Halloween costume need to be from a high performance fabric? Then, perform your own QQQ (Quick Quality Quiz) every time you buy a fabric.

QQQ (Quick Quality Quiz)

1. **Will it wrinkle?**
Perform the wrinkle test by holding a 5" square in your hand and squeeze it for five seconds. Do the wrinkles come out quickly? The higher a fiber is on the absorbency scale, the more it will wrinkle. Wovens generally wrinkle more than knits. Stretch wovens wrinkle less than regular wovens.

2. **Will it hold its shape?**
The "thumb test" can be performed by pulling a small section of the fabric with your thumbs and holding for five seconds. If it recovers quickly from the warmth and stress of your thumbs, it will hold its shape in wear. The tighter the knit or weave, the heavier the fabric, and the less absorbent the fiber, the better it will hold its shape. Generally, double knits hold their shape better than single knits, wovens better than knits, and synthetics better than natural fibers.

3. **Will it pill?**
The shorter the fiber, the more it is likely to pill. The less absorbent the fiber, the drier and more static-prone it will be and thus the short fibers will cling together, or "pill," more easily.

4. **Will it sew easily?**
Knits don't ravel, so seam finishes are unnecessary. Very stretchy fabrics and fabrics made from slippery filament fibers may be harder to handle. It's harder to press or crease nonabsorbent fibers. Nonabsorbent fibers with tight weaves pucker more readily while sewing.

5. **Will it be comfortable?**
Fabrics that are lightweight and absorbent are often more comfortable to wear. Thick knits and nonabsorbent synthetics are often warm and feel clammy. However, they wrinkle less.

TLC ... Textile Love and Care

Follow these simple guidelines for longer fabric life:

1. **Always read the bolt-end label** for fiber type and care instructions. Tape a swatch of the fabric to a file card and write fiber content and care instructions next to it for future reference.

2. **For washable fabrics,** follow these general instructions:

HOW	WHY
1. Use warm water.	1. Synthetics relax and lose wrinkles in **warm** water. Hot water may cause color loss in some.
2. Don't overcrowd washing machine.	2. Crowding causes wrinkles and abrasion, hence pilling.
3. Use detergent when preshrinking fabric.	3. Softens fabric for maximum shrinkage.
4. Avoid cold water detergents if heavily chlorinated.	4. Hard on color.
5. Use cool rinse and short spin cycle.	5. Cools fabrics so wrinkles aren't set during spin cycle.
6. Remove from washer immediately.	6. Prevents wrinkling.
7. Avoid overdrying in a dryer.	7. Causes static electricity, progressive shrinkage, and loss of fabric life.
8. Use wash and wear or permanent press dryer setting.	8. Cool-down cycle prevents wrinkling when dryer stops.
9. Remove from dryer immediately.	9. Prevents wrinkling.
10. Use fabric softener in washer or dryer, if desired	10. Helps control static electricity as well as soften fabric. If using dryer sheets, place them on top of fabrics in a **cool** dryer to avoid staining.

3. **Always preshrink as you plan to care for the finished garment.**
Preshrink shaping fabrics (see page 39) and zippers at the same time.

she said pre-shrink EVERYTHING!!!

NOTE: Save time in caring for the finished garment by leaving clothes on hangers until washed or dry-cleaned, thus minimizing wrinkling.

Exceptions

1. **Fabrics that may lose their color.**
RED, NAVY, AND BLACK. Even though they don't fade, they may seem to because of an overspray of dye. Test in sink before putting in with other clothes. Use cool water.

ACETATES. Many are dyed with less colorfast dyes. Hand wash in lots of cool water. DON'T SOAK. Line or hanger dry.

PRINTED NYLON TRICOT AND JERSEY. Color doesn't always penetrate nonabsorbent fibers. Hand wash or use a gentle, short machine cycle and cool water for longest life.

2. **100% cotton or cotton/Lycra® knits**
Preshrink three times in washer and dryer. Shrinkage may occur each time. Some shrink as much as 5" per yard.

3. **Wool**
We prefer to have wool fabrics steamed by the dry cleaner if the finished garment is going to be dry-cleaned **and** pressed by the dry cleaner. However, since we generally have our clothes "cleaned only," we don't bother to preshrink, but we do steam with a shot-of-steam type iron before cutting. So far...no trouble. Use woolens that are of good quality and "ready-for-the-needle." If you do use "washable wool," follow the manufacturer's instructions carefully. Use a "wool" cycle and **cool** water.

4. **Silk**

   Some silks are dry-clean only, so we recommend pre-shrinking these by steam pressing. Washable silks should be preshrunk in water to eliminate shrinkage **and** water spotting.

5. **Linen**

   Suit-weight linen is technically washable, but then must be ironed — **ugh!** That's like ironing heavy linen tablecloths. Life is too short, so steam press to preshrink and have the garment dry-cleaned. Blouse-weight linens can be washed.

6. **Rayon**

   Many rayons are now washable but some are not. Carefully read the bolt-end label. If washable, preshrink in the same manner the manufacturer recommends to wash. If dry-clean-only, steam to preshrink. (Test a swatch. Some can be washed, but may lose body.)

7. **Flame-retardant fabrics**

   In 1973, the federal government banned the sale of flammable children's nightwear. Initially, manufacturers treated fabrics with chemicals that reduced flammability **and** caused allergic reactions and discomfort. Many of the fabrics were stiff and boardy.

   In our first book we gave you careful laundering instructions to protect those finishes. Today, the major children's sleepwear fabric manufacturers are using fibers that are flame retardant, not finishes such as a Fortrel® polyester flannel called Flannel II. It can be machine washed in warm water but not bleached — primarily to protect the colors. The only finish applied is called Natur®. It makes the polyester more soil resistant, breathable, anti-static, and wickable. Every yard is government tested to be flame resistant, even after 50 washings. Modacrylic is another flame-retardant fiber. All-cotton flannel without a fire-retardant finish is labeled on the bolt, "not intended for children's sleepwear."

8. **Blends like rayon/polyester or cotton/Lycra** retain colors best when laundered gently. Wash in cold water using a short cycle and hang to dry. The dryer can cause abrading, pilling, and a worn out look on the surface. The 4-way stretch cotton/Lycra blended fabrics are wonderful for fitted pants and are showing up in fabric stores. They hold their shape well because they stretch in both directions.

Tools of the Trade

A craftsman is only as fine as his tools — an old but appropriate saying. Imagine what a lousy cook Julia Child might be if she had to cook dinner on a hot plate in a closet.

We really believe in investing in good quality basic tools and then splurging occasionally on some sanity-saving gadgets. Treat yourself — invest a little in your sewing now so you can sew painlessly for years to come!

The Basics

1. **Tape measure** — reinforced fiberglass won't stretch.
2. **Sewing gauge** — a 6" ruler with a sliding marker. Super for marking hems and spacing buttons. Susan has two — one at the machine and one at the ironing board.

3. **See-thru ruler** — a handy clear plastic measuring aid great for placing patterrns on fabric straight of grain and as a straight edge for marking.

4. **Tailor's chalk** — pencil or chalk with holder that has a built-in sharpening device and brush eraser is good for more permanant marking. The chalk wheel is also handy.

5. **Washable markers** — a necessity! The water-soluble pens erase when touched with a dampened cloth or cotton swab. The air-erasable ink disappears within 24 hours — sew quickly.

6. **Thimble** — Susan collects them and Pati uses them. They are great for handwork on heavy fabrics.

7. **Extra machine bobbins** — and a grooved bobbin box to hold them. Wind more than one bobbin when you begin to sew a garment.

8. **Sewing machine needles** — use a quality brand recommended for your machine and replace after 8-10 hours of stitching (or with each new garment). This will help stitch quality and prevent damage to the fabric. Types available:
   - **Universal point**, size 80/12. Most common for mid-weight fabrics.
   - **Stretch needles**, size 75/11 for most knits — cotton/Lycra®.
   - **Twin needles** to hem knits.
   - **Microtec**   • **Embroidery**
   - **Topstitching**   • **Handicap**

   There are many other needles designed for specific uses.

9. **Pins** — fine, long (1⅜") pins with large, round glass heads are easiest on the hands when pinning firm fabrics and don't melt from the heat of the iron.

10. **The Grabbit®** — another **new necessity!** We call it a marriage saver. It is a magnetic pin catcher. If your pins have fallen on the floor, hold the catcher above them and they will jump up to it!

11. **A pin cushion** — we especially like the wrist variety as it's always where you need it. A basic tomato pin cushion is also handy if you don't have a Grabbit. The attached "strawberry" sharpens pins and needles.

12. **Paper lunch bag** — tape to machine table to hold thread snips. We hate to clean house.

13. **A mug rack** — the handiest way we have found to store all those grab-for type items. If items don't have holes large enough to slip over the pegs, attach a loop of colorful ribbon.

14. **Mirror** — a full-length mirror can be found for as little as $10 and MUST be in your sewing area!

15. **Bulletin board** — above sewing machine to hold pattern pieces, needles, and pattern guidesheets.

16. **Point turner** — turns corners right side out without poking holes.

17. **Seam ripper** — be honest, you'll need it. We aren't always perfect! The small one is safest to use!

18. **7"-8" bent-handled shears** — in good condition! Have you tried the lightweights: They cut well and are **very** comfortable. Get a GOOD quality. We also like knife-edge shears! They are **very** sharp and come with a sharpening stone.

19. **Embroidery scissors** — use for clipping, snipping, and trimming. Tie them to your machine with a ribbon so they don't walk away. We also like the slightly larger tailor-point scissors for trimming and clipping heavier fabrics.

KEEP YOUR SCISSORS FOR SEWING ONLY! Have them sharpened frequently and you will smile as you sew. How can you possibly cut an elegant blouse fabric with shears your husband used to replace the porch screens?

Honey ··· I got the screen patched —
here's your scissors!

The Treats

1. **Cut 'n' Press board** — a fantastic timesaver. Place this padded cutting and pressing board on a chest of drawers at elbow height next to your sewing machine. You can steam-shrink and block to straighten off-grain fabrics on it. You can use the **large** surface for fusing interfacings in place as well as pressing as you sew. See page 13 for how it is used in Pati's sewing room. It actually replaces her ironing board. Make your own by purchasing a 36" by 54" piece of $5/8$"-thick pressed board. Put a $1/2$"-thick layer of old wool army blankets or reprocessed wool rug pad on top. Cover with muslin stapled or masking-taped to the back side. Do not use polyester batting — it is nonabsorbent.

2. **Basting tape** — a $1/8$" double-faced sewing tape used in place of pins or hand basting. Great for sewing zippers in stretchy knits.

3. **Sobo or other fabric glue** — essential for speedy basting of interfacings and underlining (unless using fusibles, of course). Not water-soluble. When used close to edges, it prevents raveling.

4. **Water soluble glue stick** — Use for glue basting. Be careful; rubbing it on bias edges can cause stretching.

5. **Pinking shears** — can be utilized in many ways besides finishing seams in ravelly fabrics. (See page 83 and 108.)

6. **An organizer tray** — for small items you can't hold on your mug rack. Keep it close to your machine. If you can't find one in a fabric store, try an office-supply store.

7. **Seam sealant** — like Fray Check™, Fray No More™ or Fray Stop, a clear liquid plastic resin used to prevent raveling. Great for corners of bound buttonholes, collar points, and to stop runs in pantyhose. Seam sealant can be removed with rubbing alcohol.

8. **Perfect Sew** — a liquid stabilizer that penetrates fabrics and stiffens them for machine embroidery. You can embroider on sheers without using any additional backing. Wash it out when finished and fabric will be as soft as it was originally.

9. **A shot-of-steam type iron** — We like the ones with lots of steam holes, a nonstick coating, and a large water container. We do not like automatic shut-off irons for sewing.

10. **Steam generator irons** — These are wonderful. They hold a lot of water, steam horizontally and vertically, and give the most steam of any iron. Some have a non-stick finish. You can continuously steam which is great for steam-shrinking woolens.

11. **Hot iron cleaner** — great for removing fusible residue from the sole plate of irons.

12. **Rotary cutter and mat** — the cutter is a circular razor-like cutting tool that looks like a pizza cutter. Use the large size for thick fabrics and the small one for tight curves. A pinking blade is now available. Place the special mat under your fabric to protect your table. Dritz has a 30"-wide mat for cutting 60" fabrics. It is ruled for easy layout. Sew Fit of La Grange, Il. has a mat that perfectly fits their cardboard cutting tables.

A ~~Few Thoughts~~ Dissertation On Thread

With so many different types of thread available today, confusion is understandable. We hope we can answer a few of your questions.

All-purpose polyester thread — can be used on virtually any fabric. Whether you choose polyester or polyester-core cotton-wrapped thread, you will have a thread that doesn't shrink or fade, is strong, and gives to be compatible with knits. There is a difference in the quality of threads — a "bargain" thread may create fabric and machine headaches. Look for a thread that is smooth, even, fine, and strong.

Long-staple polyester thread — 4 to 5½" fibers are used in place of 1½" fibers for spinning the threads. This produces a superior quality thread that has improved hand-sewing ability, greater luster, and extra strength. It is also more expensive, so we save it for finer fabrics like silk or polyester silkies where luster and sewability are important.

Serger thread — Because so much thread is used in serged seams and seam finishes, serger thread is slightly finer than all-purpose thread. Serger thread has a special finish applied to make it extra smooth for high-speed sewing. It is sold in cones or tubes of 1,000 to 1,500 yards for greater economy. It is not recommended for regular sewing machine use because it would be weaker in a straight stitched-seam.

Extra-fine polyester thread — Coats & Clark makes a great cotton-wrapped polyester thread that is finer than any of the above so it is ideal for lingerie and lightweight fabrics.

Polyester topstitching thread — used for decorative topstitching. This is a fat thread and needs a larger needle eye to pass through to keep it from shredding. Use a large machine needle, size 16 or 18, or try a topstitching needle. Different machines will tolerate thicker thread in different ways. Try all three methods before you insist your machine won't sew with these threads:

1. Topstitching thread on top, all-purpose thread in the bobbin — the most common combination.

2. Regular thread on top, topstitching thread in the bobbin.

3. Topstitching thread on top **and** in the bobbin.

Silk buttonhole twist — a heavy silk thread originally used for handworked buttonholes and now used for decorative topstitching. Though difficult to find, this elegant thread with its subtle sheen is well worth the extra cost.

Cotton thread — has limited give and is not as strong as polyester thread. It may shrink so is not recommended for low-shrink synthetic fabrics. However, cotton thread sews well, dyes beautifully, and has a lovely luster that is great for machine embroidery. Good selections are often available at sewing machine stores.

Silk sewing thread — made from protein, so it sews well on protein fabrics like silk and wool. Silk thread is quite strong and elastic, yet still very fine. It is ideal for basting, and for sewing very fine silk fabrics.

Thread color

Pati was a very frustrated buyer for a sewing notions department when she found her customers **always** insisting upon "perfect" thread match for **every** fabric. We like to use matching threads whenever possible, but we certainly don't drive to 76 stores nor lose sleep over it if we can't match it perfectly. Generally, choose thread a shade darker as it will appear lighter off the spool as it sews in. If a perfect match for topstitching is not possible, select the following:

1. a shade lighter for a dressier and more elegant effect
2. a shade darker for a sportier look.
3. a complete contrast for a very casual appearance.

    With serger thread, the color selection is much more limited and the investment greater because of cone size, so we use "blending" colors. A friend uses only gray serger thread, feeling that it blends in tone with all fabrics. Only the needle thread penetrates the fabric, so match it if you can. The looper threads do not need to match.

The Biggie

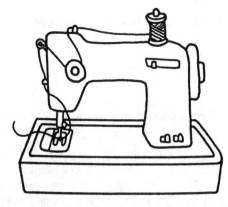

Investing in a sewing machine may be one of your **larger** expenditures, so take time to make the right choice. Machines are like people; they have individual personalities. Be sure to try several brands to see which suits you best. Some dealers have a home trial program and some "rent-with-option-to-buy." So do test — you wouldn't buy a car without a test drive, would you?

We would prefer to suggest a top-of-the-line machine in any brand, because it does everything but sing to us. But is it really the best choice for **you**? The woman who plans to do no more than patch jeans and make decorator pillows does not **need** that much machine. It would be like buying a Porsche and letting it sit in the garage.

One of our pet peeves is a beginning seamstress (or her husband) buying a $3000 machine when she isn't even sure she wants to sew. Know your needs and budget and then shop to find out all the options available before making your choice. If the $3000 machine is easier for you to operate (and you need all the help you can get), then that alone might justify it. If you are **really** confused, consider the following guidelines. Are you...

1. **A beginner** — you have never sewed before, not sure if you'll even like it, but need something to sew on. Look for the best basic machine you can afford, an "entry-level" model from a solid manufacturer or a used model. As your skills and interests grow, you can trade up later or keep the machine for your children. Avoid off-brand or unusually cheap machines, whose unreliability alone could turn you off to sewing.

2. **Someone who has been sewing for some time** — you really like your old machine, but want something new. If you don't already own a serger, buy one as a companion to your old machine to increase your sewing speed and upgrade the quality. When it comes to replacing your old sewing machine, shop around and learn all you can about current features. An electronic machine will offer you convenience features, such as automatic needle stop and electronic foot control, while a computerized model includes easier stitch selection and memory buttonholes, not to mention much more versatility.

3. **One who loves to sew, sew constantly,** tries all the new patterns and fabrics and wants the "ultimate" in a machine. You are a "top-of-the-line" customer if your wallet allows. For $2,000 or more, you will get a computerized machine with an abundance of built-in stitches. Even if you'd never use *half* the stitches available, you still may find investment in a top model to be worthwhile for its extra ease-of-operation features. As you move up the price range to that "ultimate" machine, you will find seemingly unlimited decorative possibilities, including even a computer interface that allows you to "design" your own stitches.

No matter what machine you buy, discipline yourself to learn all its features. Take any lessons the machine dealer offers. Insist on an instruction manual(s) with any new or used machine, and ask about instructional videos. And then **practice**! Master all the options your new machine offers, and you'll discover a "new way to sew" that is easier and maybe even more creative and fun.

Read your manual and follow the care instructions completely. Keep the machine lint-free and oiled, and have it serviced annually by a reputable sewing machine dealer. Between uses, don't hide your machine away in a cabinet; keep it set up so you can use it whenever you have spare minutes. Use a folding screen if you need to hide your sewing corner.

Where to Buy Your Machine

Selecting the right dealer is important, especially if you are buying an expensive machine. Find someone you like and can trust, who offers lessons on the use of the machine and who can service it over the years. If you buy a serger to go along with your conventional machine, a good dealer who services is even more important as sergers must be in **perfect** timing to sew well!

Features Your Sewing Machine May Not Have

Since many of you may be living with the machine mom gave you or one you bought 30 years ago, we should tell you what features we like on newer machines.

1. **Needle can stop up or down.** If you are topstitching, have it stop down so the needle is in the fabric when you pivot around a corner.

2. **Slow/fast speed.** When Pati's 9-year-old daughter sews, the machine is set in the slow position.

3. **The needle can move to the left or right in very small increments.** This is nice for more perfect piping, zipper sewing, topstitching and perfect ¼" seams in quilts.

4. **Truly automatic buttonholes.** These can be programmed to repeat the same length buttonhole continuously. There are several types — those with an "electric eye," those where you put your button tight in the buttonhole attachment, and those strictly computerized. In many, both sides will look the same because they zigzag forward on one side, straight stitch backward on the other side and zigzag over the straight stitching. With the zigzag going forward on both sides, stitches are more even in density. Take a variety of fabrics to the dealer and YOU try out the buttonhole on a machine you'd like to buy. Technology changes rapidly.

5. **Automatic tension.** Most electronic and computer machines have this. From our experience, it works very well.

6. **Snap on presser feet.** These are real time savers and work very well in most cases. However, Pati bought a dream machine — top of the line — and was pleasantly surprised to see they've maintained the best old zipper foot she has ever used. It screws on and the foot slides back and forth. New is not always best, this company admitted.

7. **Cuts both threads next to fabric** at beginning and end of a seam with the touch of a button. This is a wonderful feature. Watch as more and more machines get this.

Most of us with free-arm machines do all of our sewing with the free-arm exposed. However, many machines are now coming with an extension that fits around the free-arm that also has an accessory compartment. THREE CHEERS FOR THOSE MANUFACTURERS.

Now, if you can't afford a new sewing machine, at least invest in a serger. If you have an old straight stitch machine and are happy with it, put your money into the machine that can finish your seams and do much more. See our book *Sewing With Sergers* for buying ideas.

Lastly, if you do buy a new machine or serger, hang onto your old one for classes, your children, or to have one always threaded with white thread.

Sergers or Overlock Machines

The serger, also called an overlock machine, has revolutionized sewing. It stitches, trims and overcasts in one step at almost twice the speed of a conventional sewing machine.

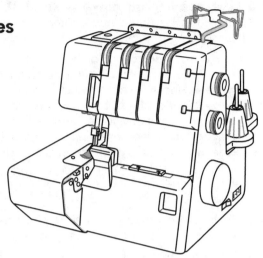

Even though there are some garments that can be sewn **entirely** on the serger, most of the time you will use a combination of your conventional machine and your serger. They make a perfect pair. Think of it this way . . . did you toss your knives when you bought your food processor?

Sergers are used on both knit and woven fabrics, and can be used to finish conventional seam edges or to stitch, cut, and overcast a narrow seam in one step.

conventional seam finish   *narrow serged seam*

Each stitch is "knitted" by needle(s) and loopers over a "stitch finger." This metal prong keeps the fabric flat during stitch formation, preventing the threads from drawing up the edge of even the lightest weight fabric.

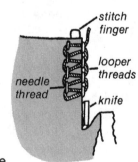

stitch finger
looper threads
needle thread
knife

See our book *Sewing With Sergers* for detailed information on these fascinating machines. (See page 127.)

Quick Shaping

Since the first writing of *Painless Sewing* in 1975, shaping fabrics have changed dramatically. Technology has gone forward by leaps and bounds and those early products have been replaced by sophisticated ones that perform to very high standards. **We do not have to give up quality for speed** — now even the most discriminating ready-to-wear manufacturers use fusibles successfully.

Since our first edition, our chapter on interfacings and other shaping fabrics has also changed a great deal. As fashion has changed, so has the need for so many inside layers. In 1975, interfacing, lining, and underlining were all used in the same garment. Now fashion is less structured and more flowing. Guess what — sewing is easier than ever!

Lining — a layer of fabric cut and sewn separately from the fashion fabric. It covers inside construction, makes jackets easier to slip on and wear, prevents bagging in skirts and pants.

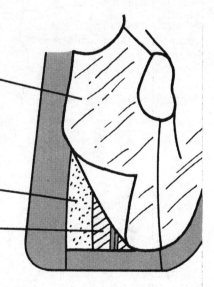

Interfacing — a stabilizing layer used to prevent stretching and add body to garment edges and to detail areas like collars, cuffs, and closures.

Underlining — a layer of fabric cut from the same pattern pieces as the fashion fabric. These layers are sewn together and then treated as one in all seams. Underlining provides shape, body and support to large areas.

To Interface or Not To Interface

When in doubt, interface! Most things look terrific when brand new, but interfaced garments still look great years later. Garments without interfacings develop the "saggies" much faster.

No matter what interfacing you choose, it will be better than if you used nothing. Even soft fabrics and soft styles may need soft interfacings in areas of extra strain to prevent a droopy look. Also, different garments receive different types of wear. We interface the hem of a coat or jacket because it gets a tremendous amount of strain, but not the hem of a dress. In an evening dress we plan to wear once, we interface for appearance only, not for durability.

Where To Use Interfacings

Edges — because edges are subject to excessive wear and interfacings provide strength, body, and stretch prevention in these areas.

Neckline needs help because it supports the entire garment.

Armhole needs help because of perspiration wear.

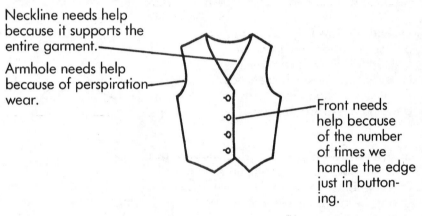

Front needs help because of the number of times we handle the edge just in buttoning.

collar detail

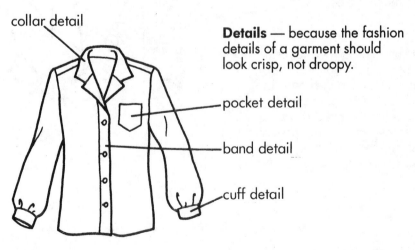

Details — because the fashion details of a garment should look crisp, not droopy.

pocket detail

band detail

cuff detail

How to Choose an Interfacing

Welcome to the world of confusion! There are so many inter-facings out there, we get nothing but cries of help. Therefore, in this chapter, we will give you all the latest information that will help you make good decisions. But, if all else fails, find a fabric store with experienced sewers as salespeople. They can give you good advice. Also, remember that fashion influences how firm or soft the interfacing should be. There are four basic categories of fabrics used for interfacings and each category includes both stitchables and fusibles.

Fusible Interfacings

We suggest using fusible interfacings whenever possible. They give the best look in the least amount of time. Today's fusibles can be used with nearly every fabric because of the new fusible resins. The original fusibles had a polyethyline resin (plastic bag material) in the form of granules that were melted with a dry iron. We called them the "bake-ons." They usually came off after the first washing. Today's fusibles use primarily polyamide resins applied to the inter-facing with calendaring or computer-dot methods and are fused with steam.

Stitchable Interfacings

Even though we highly recommend fusible interfacings, there is still a place in fine sewing for stitchables. Because a fusible becomes somewhat firmer after application, a stitchable may give you a softer, more subtle shape. Fusibles cannot be used with some fabrics like velvet and velveteen, or with fabrics with extreme surface texture like seersucker or crinkly gauze. Fusing will flatten most of these fabrics and drastically change their surface character. Also, fusibles won't adhere to fabrics with a high triacetate fiber content. Stitchables are always safe with any fabric, important if you are unable to test fusibles with your fabric first.

Woven stitchables work in both woven and knit fabrics. Nonwoven stitchables may "buckle" in enclosed areas such as collars in woven fabrics. They don't contract with the fabric, but they can expand or stretch. This makes them especially compatible in collars of knit garments or in any area where give is desirable.

"Help! There Are Too Many Interfacings!"

We hear this all of the time. But don't let interfacing selection become a big deal. Trust us! Shop, test, and discover your favorites.

Remember, serious seamstresses should have their own "interfacing store" at home. Preshrink and label each so they are ready to use. We often use more than one interfacing in each garment. We also often use double layers — a lightweight interfacing on the top collar and a medium weight on the under collar, for example.

Here Are the Ones We Use the Most

Lightweight weft-insertion fusibles — Weft-insertion interfacings are actually knits with a yarn woven in the weft (crosswise) direction that have the drapability of a knit and the crosswise stability of a woven. Lightweight polyester weft interfacings work well on lightweight silkies because they virtually never bubble or pucker after washing. Use one or two layers in collars and cuffs. They are crisper than fusible knits. They also work very well on preshrunk cotton and poly/cotton shirtings. Polyester weft interfacings don't need to be preshrunk.

Some of these lightweight weft interfacings are for underlining or fusing to textured surfaces. These usually have a more open weave.

Medium and heavy weft-insertion fusibles — These usually have a rayon content and make excellent tailoring interfacings. Usually the medium weight is used on a jacket upper collar and facing and the heavier on the front and under collar. These should be preshrunk.

Fusible knits — These are ideal for fusing to all pieces in an unlined jacket made out of a lightweight fabric. They add body, won't snag, and are slippery like a lining. We usually don't fuse to the sleeve as it can make the jacket too hot in a warm climate. Steam shrink fusible knits. They also work well in silky blouse fabrics, though we find the polyester wefts a little crisper.

Silk organza — This is great in a fabric you can't fuse to like seersucker or velvet. We also use it to make window-pane bound buttonholes. Cut on the bias, it faces the hole under which the lips are placed. Preshrink if you are planning to wash the finished garment.

Medium weight sew-in non-woven — this is a must under welt pockets. See the technique for Goof-proof Super Duper Double Welt Pockets in our tailoring book (see page 128).

Poly/cotton sew-in wovens — We use this type of woven fabric across the back of a jacket. Fusibles will often leave a line across the shoulder blades, if not immediately, after a few cleanings.

Non-woven fusibles — We often use the ones with give or all-bias in knits.

Polyester tie interfacing or polyester fleece — We use tie interfacing cut on the bias or the stretchier cross grain of fleece as a sleeve head. Sew strips of either to the sleeve cap in a jacket for a firm, rounded look.

Waistband interfacing — Monofilament nylon won't roll. (See page 127.)

Preshrinking Interfacings

You will need to test interfacings before selecting the one you want to use. If your garment is washable, you should preshrink **both** your fabric and interfacing for realistic test results. Today's interfacings have only a 1-2% shrinkage factor, but your fashion fabric may have more or less. Therefore, we recommend preshrinking for safety. A real advantage to sewing is that you can pretreat your fabrics and put an end to ugly bubbling you've seen in ready-mades after laundering.

Preshrinking Fusibles

Woven, weft, and knit fusibles — Place in a basin of HOT water and soak for 20 minutes. It will not hurt the fusing agent, which is activated at 300 degrees or more. Do not agitate or you might dislodge some of the fusing resin. Blot in a towel and hang over a towel rack to dry. **Do not wad up or wring. Do not machine dry!** There is one exception, **a polyester weft does not need preshrinking**.

Nonwoven fusibles — There is no need to preshrink in water. If these shrink at all, it is the steam from your iron that causes it. Try "steam shrinking." Place your interfacing on your fabric. Hold your iron 2" above the interfacing and steam for three or four seconds in each area. You will actually see some interfacings shrink while steaming. A "shot-of-steam" type of iron works best.

Preshrinking Stitchables

Woven stitchables — Most have only a 1-2% shrinkage factor. However, it is best to preshrink to assure compatibility with your preshrunk fashion fabric. Preshrink in the same method you plan to clean the finished garment. If washing, use detergent. If drycleaning your finished garment, generally heavily steaming the interfacing is adequate.

Non-woven stitchables — Simply steam the interfacing before attaching to your fashion fabric.

Testing Interfacings

The key to successful interfacing is to **TEST. Fusibles get firmer** after fusing and **stitchables get softer** after washing. You can't test interfacings in a fabric store! Therefore, we recommend having your own **interfacing store** at home. Keep on hand a selection of several weights of fusibles and stitchables.

Buy 2-3 yards of each that you commonly use and cut off only what you need each time. (One yard is adequate if the interfacings are 60" wide.) **You'll save money** on gas since you won't need to drive to the fabric store for every garment! **Save time also** by going directly from the fabric store to the bathroom sink and preshrinking all those interfacings requiring it. Then all your interfacings will be "ready" when you are.

How to Test Fusibles

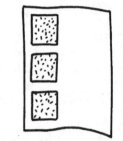

Cut 3-4" squares of several different types, weights, and colors of interfacings you are considering. Preshrink interfacing and fabric if appropriate. Pink one edge of interfacing if fusing only part of a piece to see if the edge will blend into the fabric and disappear.

Fuse to a scrap of fabric wide enough to fold over the interfacing. This enables you to feel the interfacing between two layers of fashion fabric. The pinked edge should not leave a line on the right side.

If the finished garment will be washed, wash your test sample. Check for puckers and "strike-through" (see page 41).

How to Test Stitchables

Preshrink interfacing and fabric if the finished garment is washable. Sandwich the interfacing between two layers of fashion fabric. **Feel** the layers together. Do they have the amount of body you want in an edge or detail area?

Does your interfacing show through too much? – The lingerie guideline applies here. A color close to your skin color shows the least. Or, blend with the main color of the sheer using black or white.

Common Problems with Fusibles

Since we began to use fusibles in the late 1960s, we have had our share of disasters including fusing to the iron! However, as the products improved and we gained more experience, we developed solutions to the following problems.

Puckering or bubbling — usually caused by one fabric shrinking more than the other. If the fashion fabric bubbles, the interfacing has shrunk. If the interfacing bubbles, the fashion fabric has shrunk. Bubbling shows up most on smooth, tightly woven fabrics and on silkies.

ALL RIGHT..... NOW WHAT DO YOU DO NEXT ?

Strike-through — when the fusing agent shows through to the right side of your fabric, creating an ugly polka-dot appearance. Sometimes this doesn't happen until after many launderings or drycleanings. To avoid the possibility on lightweight sheer fabrics, use an interfacing designed for sheers.

Interfacing won't stick — some fusibles don't adhere well to surfaces that are nubby, napped, or fuzzy like wool tweeds and corduroy. When interfacing corduroy, cut interfacing so that the stable direction is perpendicular to the rows of wales. If a fabric is very smooth and tightly woven, interfacings resist bonding. It will take more time to get a decent fuse.

Interfacing leaves a line on the right side — try pinking the edge that shows. It will blend right in with the fabric. If it doesn't, cut the interfacing to a dart stitching line or interface the entire piece.

How to Use Fusibles

Cutting

We used to trim ½" from the edges of fusible interfacings so that only ⅛" was caught in the seam. This eliminated bulk. This is no longer necessary with the new softer and lighter weight fusibles. However, we do like to have the interfacing a little smaller than the fabric piece to keep from getting any fusible residue on our ironing board. Using a collar as an example, our easy way of doing is shown on the next page.

1. Cut the long edge first.

2. Next cut one of the short edges.

3. Slide the pattern piece until the stitching lines on the long and short edges of the pattern piece are on the edges you just cut.

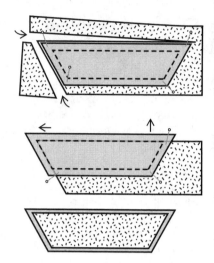

3. Finish cutting.

4. Re-center pattern to see the results. VOILA! The interfacing is slightly smaller.

Fusing

1. Preheat iron set to "WOOL" or low steam setting.

2. Steam press fashion fabric to remove any wrinkles and to allow for any shrinkage caused by steam.

3. Place pattern back on fabric to make sure the fabric has not gotten distorted.

4. Place resin side of interfacing on wrong side of fashion fabric.

5. Use a press cloth to prevent fusible residue from getting on your iron, especially with the lightweight fusibles. If you don't have a shot-of-steam type iron, use a dampened press cloth.

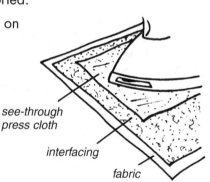

see-through press cloth

interfacing

fabric

NOTE: We love the steam generator irons. We've been spoiled. They steam in any direction, even upside down. They produce continuous steam created in a large capacity water tank on which the iron rests. Due to the vents being primarily in the front of the iron, always fuse moving the iron forward so the dry part of the iron is heating the part you just steamed.

6. Fuse 5-10 seconds, lift and move iron 2-3"; fuse another 5-10 seconds. Continue this way, overlapping as you go, making sure all areas of interfacing are pressed 10-15 seconds total. Lightweight fabrics and fusibles require less fusing time, generally 10 seconds. Heavier interfacings and fabrics can take up to 25 seconds. TEST!!! Susan uses the **Mississippi** trick to count seconds. One Mississippi, two Mississippi, three Mississippi, etc. Better yet, have a clock with a second hand in your sewing area.

7. Use FIRM, two handed pressure. Overlap pressed areas to ensure complete fusing.

8. **Be patient!** Always allow fused pieces to cool **before** moving.

The Perfect Fuse™ Solution

Palmer/Pletsch has developed four fusible weft interfacings—Perfect Fuse Sheer, Light, Medium and Tailor. We had several goals:

- **Simplification.** There are so many interfacing choices that the customer has no idea what to use where. We narrowed the choices to only four that will solve nearly every interfacing need.

- **To be able to see the difference.** Often, you can't tell the difference visually between one interfacing and another. These four are distinctly different.

- **Good performance.** Some interfacings bubble during laundering or abrade and pill. These are wefts which perform superiorly. They add stability as well as softness. In-depth care and preshrinking instructions are included in the package.

- **Wider widths.** These new interfacings are 60 and 66 inches wide, TWICE the width of most other interfacings, which must be pieces in some garments.

- **Good instructions.** Each of the new interfacings has its own instructions. In addition, each package includes well-researched and well-written general instructions for using fusibles.

- **Less confusion in your interfacing stash at home.** Often, after we use an interfacing, we stack it on the shelf and three months later we can't figure out what it is. These come in a protective storage bags that keep the interfacing clean and identifiable.

- **Quality.** Consumers aren't very confident in how interfacings will perform. We tested hundreds of products over a four-year period and spent two years writing, editing, and testing use and care instructions.

TYPE & FIBER	FABRICS	CARE	USES
Example: Perfect Fuse Sheer polyester wefts 60" wide	◆ Smooth-surfaced semi-sheer to lightweight synthetics and blends such as rayon, silk, fine microfiber, cotton shirting, tissue faille, and semi-sheer blouse fabrics	◆ Preshrinking NOT required ◆ Finished garment is machine washable and machine dryable if fashion fabric is also machine washable and machine dryable. If not, line dry. ◆ Dry cleanable* Ⓟ	◆ Pockets ◆ Hems (cut on bias) ◆ Facings ◆ Collars, bands & cuffs ◆ Upper collar and facing on a jacket when just a little extra body is needed ◆ Underlining: Light to give body to lightweight fabrics
Example: Perfect Fuse Light, Texture Weft polyester wefts	◆ Textured surfaces that are woven ◆ Lightweight to medium weight knits ◆ Can be made of synthetic fibers, blends, or all natural fibers. Examples are crepe, silk noil, fine-wale corduroy, cotton flannel, and crinkle rayon.		
Example: Perfect Fuse Medium, Whisper Weft rayon and polyester wefts	◆ Any dress- or jacket-weight fabric when you need more body than PerfectFuse Light and less than the heavier PerfectFuse Tailor. It is a good choice for Ultrasuede® and Ultrasuede Light.®	◆ Preshrink by soaking in hot water 10 min. and line drying. ◆ Finished garment may be GENTLY hand or machine washed depending on fashion fabric fiber content. Line dry. ◆ Dry cleanable* Ⓟ	Tailored jackets: fuse a test sample to determine the best weight. ◆ Medium is usually used on upper collar and facings and cut on the bias in jacket hems. ◆ Tailor is used on under collar and entire jacket front. ◆ Pockets
Example: Perfect Fuse Tailor, Armoweft rayon and polyester wefts	◆ Tailoring-weight fabrics including wool flannel, crepe, tweed, gabardine, and doubleknit. Also use with silk suiting, linen and coatings. Use when your fabric needs lots of body but a soft hand.		

*For dry cleaning, use any solvent except trichloroethylene.

See page 127 for Perfect Fuse.

How to Use Stitchables

Basting an interfacing in place is tedious and not always accurate. There is too much chance of the interfacing slipping while sewing.

What is the answer? — GLUING

With what? — SOBO GLUE! Sobo is a fabric glue that dries fairly clear and soft. It can be found in most sewing-notion departments or art supply stores.

Where do you glue? — On the very edge of the seam allowance using small dots of Sobo.

1. Press the two layers together.

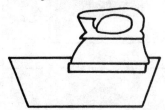

2. Lightly dot glue on seam allowances every 1-2" and pat together. It **will not wash out**, so put it only on the very edge.

3. Let dry. It takes about five minutes.

4. How do you unglue? Reheat the glue dots with an iron for three seconds and gently pull apart.

NOTE: How do you get glue out if you goofed and didn't follow instructions and glued inside the seam allowance? You don't! **We have tried everything.** PLEASE...be careful!

Where to Apply Interfacings

In small areas, both stitchables and fusibles can be applied to the side that shows. In a large area, the fusible interfacings are generally applied to the underside such as to a facing. Use the following as a guide.

	FUSIBLES	**STITCHABLES (GLUEABLES)**
Shirt/ blouse/ dress collar	*upper* *May also fuse to under collar.*	*upper*
Cuff	*upper* — *fold* *May also fuse to entire cuff.*	*upper* — *fold*
Blouse or dress front	*fold*	*fold*
Vest front	*facing* *facing* *May also fuse to entire front.*	

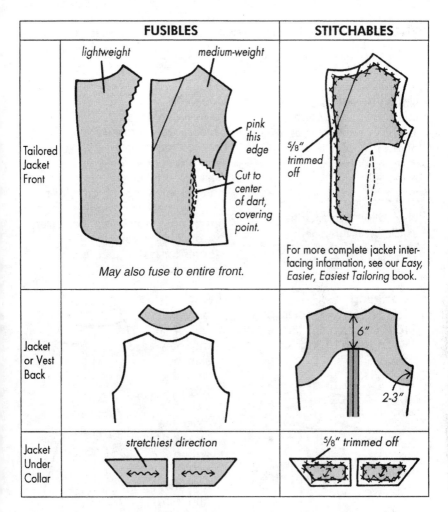

	FUSIBLES	STITCHABLES
Tailored Jacket Front	*lightweight* *medium-weight* pink this edge Cut to center of dart, covering point. *May also fuse to entire front.*	⅝" trimmed off For more complete jacket interfacing information, see our *Easy, Easier, Easiest Tailoring* book.
Jacket or Vest Back		6" 2-3"
Jacket Under Collar	*stretchiest direction*	⅝" trimmed off

Linings and Underlinings

Underlinings are sewed into the seams with the fashion fabric, and linings are sewed separately and attached only on the edges. The following are reasons you might choose to underline or line a garment:

1. To prevent seams and underwear from showing through light colors. Underlining does this best as it also cushions seam allowances.
2. To keep wools from itching or scratching. Lining gives the most complete coverage. It also helps jackets slip on and off more easily.
3. To strengthen loosely woven or fragile fabrics. Underlining works best because it is sewn into all seams with the outer fabric.
4. To prevent baggy pant knees and skirt seats. Underlining is best for same reason as above.
5. To prevent wrinkling — either will do the job.

47

Underline with...

Cotton or poly/cotton
  batiste or silk organza
Polyester lining
Ambiance® (rayon)
China silk

For more body...
Poly/cotton broadcloth
Fusible weft interfacing
Hair canvas for structure

Line with...

Polyester linings or
  blouse-weight fabrics
Poly/cotton batiste
Ambiance® (rayon)
Acetate coat lining
Hang Free® (very soft anti-static
      polyester, 54" wide)
Hang Loose® (anti-static polyester)
Silk or silky polyester
  (prints for a designer touch)
China silk

Underlining

1. Cut underlining using pattern for garment. Baste to wrong side of fashion fabric.

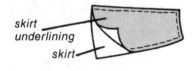

2. Sew skirt, treating the two layers as one.

Lining

1. Sew skirt out of lining. Sew skirt out of fashion fabric.

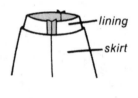
lining
skirt

2. Place the two skirts wrong sides together and join them at waist and hem.

Underlinings are "Glueable"

The "Glue and Fold" Technique

When a garment is on your body, it is not on a flat surface like it is when on the table. When on your body, these two layers form a cylinder. If they are glued together on a flat surface, they will look like this when on the body:

With the "glue and fold" method, we make the inside cylinder slightly smaller like this:

48

Underlining a Skirt Using the "Glue and Fold" Technique

Use Sobo or another fabric glue that dries soft and flexible. Don't use glue stick as it will stretch the edges when rubbed on. Sobo is permanent, so use only on seam allowances.

1. Cut underlining and fashion fabric from the same pattern piece.

2. Mark darts on underlining only.

3. Steam press the two layers together to remove wrinkles and excess shrinkage caused by steam.

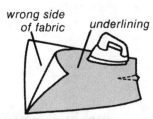

wrong side of fabric   underlining

4. Lift edges of underlining and dab **small** glue dots on to seam allowances. Pat the two layers together.

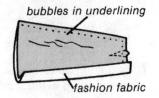

wrong side of fabric   underlining

5. Quickly, before glue dries, fold the skirt in half lengthwise toward center front or back. A bubble will form in underlining.

6. Fold again and the bubble will get larger.

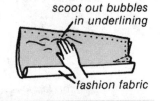

bubbles in underlining

fashion fabric

7. Scoot excess underlining (the bubble) off the edge while glue is still wet. Let dry for five minutes in rolled position.

scoot out bubbles in underlining

fashion fabric

NOTE: There is no need to trim off the excess underlining unless it gets in your way. Actually it is best to leave it as an extra cushion for the seams. Or, you can serge it off during edge finishing.

8. After glue dries, baste through center of dart, ½" past dart point to catch both layers when stitching dart.

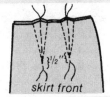

skirt front

NOTE: The dart may have moved a small amount toward the center. It's not enough to worry about.

9. Sew skirt together, treating the two
   layers as one. When you turn up
   the hem, the underlining will scoot
   out a bit as another inner cylinder
   is created. This is why we don't
   glue the hem edge.

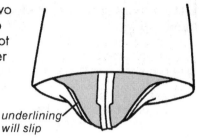

underlining
will slip

Rules and Exceptions to Glue and Fold

1. As a "very general" rule of thumb, we fold once for every seam.
   Fold each skirt piece twice. Fold each sleeve twice. Fold each pant
   leg twice.

trim off
excess

2. You can "quick check" to see if it is too large by taking the garment
   and folding in the seam allowances as if they had been pressed and
   sewed and curving the section into a half moon. Does the curve use
   up all the excess?

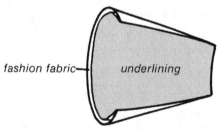

fashion fabric — underlining

3. Where you are flat and there are no seam allowances pressed
   in, don't fold at all. For example, across the upper back or chest
   of a garment with set-in sleeves there is no need to fold because
   the fabric will be flat in that area and the sleeve seam allowance
   goes into the sleeve. However, it would be difficult to fold twice
   below the armhole if you aren't folding at all above; so just fold
   once even though there are two seam allowances.

4. For any garment with small vertical sections, once is enough. Each gore in an eight-gored skirt or an eight-gored blazer is pretty narrow. Fold once only.

5. If an upper collar or yoke is underlined, fold horizontally once.

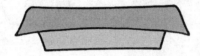

Special Tips for a Lined Skirt

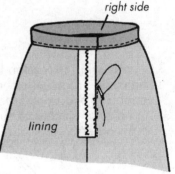

right side

lining

1. After attaching waistband, hand slipstitch lining to zipper tape.

2. The lining should always be cut the length of finished garment. When turned up it will ALWAYS be shorter than the garment and not show.

3. A "jump hem" is a tidy way to finish lined skirt. Hem garment first, then turn under lining to desired length and pin about one inch away from fold. Fold lining back to pins and slip stitch lining to skirt hem with a long hemming stitch. Be sure to catch only lining hem allowance and not lining itself.

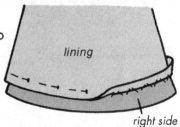

lining

right side

NOTE: Other options for hemming skirt linings are to finish the edge with a narrow rolled edge on a serger or to narrow hem on a conventional machine and let the lining hang loose from the skirt.

A Nifty Lining Technique — A Flip Lined Vest

1. Make lining smaller by trimming ⅛" from neck, armholes, and front. (This keeps lining from showing when vest is finished.)

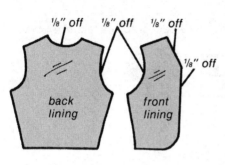

2. Sew darts and shoulder seams in both lining and fashion fabric.

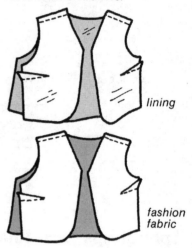

3. Match lining to fashion fabric right sides together at neck, armholes and front. Stitch using small stitches at curves and corners.

4. Trim, grade, and press the seams you have just sewed. Also clip, notch, and slash where necessary. Trim curved seams with pinking shears.

5. Turn vest to right side by reaching through back shoulders and pulling vest fronts through.

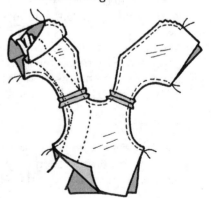

NOTE: Press thoroughly before sewing side seams. Press shoulder and neck areas over a ham. **Anchor by pinning into ham**.

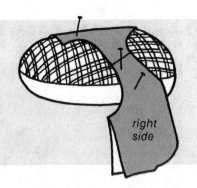

right side

6. Sew side seams by matching underarm seams. Sew lining front and back right sides together and fashion fabric front and back right sides together at side seams. Press side seams open.

7. After side seams are stitched, turn wrong side out through opening at bottom.

opening

8. Stitch across bottom. Leave a 5" opening. Trim seam.

NOTE: Machine baste across 5" opening. Snip basting thread to form opening.

wrong side

5"

9. Turn vest through the 5" opening and press bottom edge. Slipstitch the opening closed.

NOTE: You **may** cut a strip of fusible web and fuse the opening closed.

In our book *Sew A Beautiful Wedding* we use this same basic technique to sew a lined sleeveless top or dress.

Pretty Pati's Perfect Pattern Primer

"I'll just make it fit!"

Pretty Pati's Perfect Pattern Primer

We chose this wording for the sake of alliteration, but we were serious about the importance of emphasizing good fit as a part of good sewing. The finest quality fabric and the best workmanship cannot compensate for poor fit. In fact, 25% of your sewing time should be spent fitting. Use *Fit For Real People* (see back of this book, page 127).

Standards of Good Fit

1. The garment is neither too tight nor too loose.
2. The crosswise grain at bust and hip is parallel to the floor.
3. The side seams are perpendicular to the floor and in the center of the leg.
4. The shoulder seams are in the center of the shoulders.
5. The top of a set-in sleeve is at the pivot bone.
6. There are **no** wrinkles "pointing to fit problems."
7. Darts point to fullness, but stop short of the fullest part.

Fashion Changes the Standards

Armholes can be large or close-fitting. Shoulders can be broad, cut in, squared with shoulder pads, or natural. Pants can be full through the hips or fitted. Darts come and go depending on the latest silhouette.

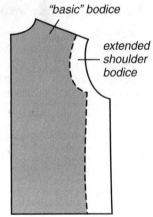

"basic" bodice

extended shoulder bodice

The nice thing about fashion is that sometimes a fit problem **suddenly disappears**! This happens most when fashion is oversized. For example, when fashion shows a squared extended shoulder, the size and position of the armhole is changed. Notice the extra ease in the bodice as well.

In this chapter we are going to tell you how to...

1. BUY THE RIGHT SIZE PATTERN
2. TISSUE FIT
3. CUT-TO-FIT
4. FIT-AS-YOU-SEW

To make this **all** easy, you first need to **get to know your body**.

Get to Know Your Body

You will never know how to fit unless you get to know your body. Here are a few hints to help you get to know your body better. Remember, **be honest**! . . . cheating now is like cheating at solitaire!

Get a Full-Length Mirror

Do you own one now?

_____ If yes, you get 5 points.

_____ If it is in your sewing area you get 10 points. Yes, **ten**! When you look in the mirror, note the shape of your body. It is caused by either **genetics** or **gravity** or both.

Genetics

Because of genetics, you are born with a certain shape and body proportions. The way your body changes over the years is also related to genetics.

Shape

The following are common body shapes:

Hourglass—⧗
balanced
hip and
shoulder
width with a
defined waist.

Triangle— △
narrow
shoulders
in compar-
ison to hips.

**Inverted ▽
triangle—**
wide shoul-
ders in com-
parison to
hips.

Rectangle—▯
little or
no waist
indentation.

Our book *Clothes Sense* tells you how to make a "body graph." This is an easy way to see your shape and proportions. Make one if you have a hard time visualizing your body.

Another example of shape is shoulder slope. You are born with average, sloping, or square shoulders.

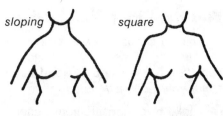

sloping   *square*

Proportion

Proportion is the length of the different body sections. Three people standing in a row may all be the same size and height, but vary in waist and leg length.

"... but we're all 5'4" and wear a size 12!"

NOTE: Proportioned patterns are not necessarily the answer for a tall or short person. The cartoon lady on the right would have a tight crotch if she bought a pant pattern proportioned for petites. Find out **where** you are long or short and buy a **regular** pattern and lengthen or shorten it in the right places.

Gravity

When our "svelte figure" changes, we blame it on **gravity**!

- A flat derriere. If you are over 25, gravity may have taken its toll and caused your derriere to drop . . . or **disappear!**

- A lower bustline. It dropped, too! The no-bra or soft bra looks help gravity along.

- Round shoulders. This can be caused by poor posture.

- A low shoulder and a high hip. **Cause** — carrying books, babies, or groceries on one side only.

57

Buy the Right Size Pattern

Fitting is easier if you **start** with the right size pattern. Yet many people buy the wrong size. Patterns are made for the average B bra cup size. If you are a DD and buy according to your bust measurement, your pattern will be too large in the neck and shoulder area.

Take **two** measurements, chest or "high bust" (A) and full bust (B). If the difference is 2½" or more, substitute the "high bust" measurement for "bust" on the measurement chart when buying patterns. If the pattern is then too tight in the bustline, make the large-bust adjustment shown on page 70.

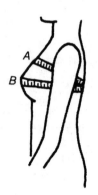

> **NOTE:** Measure **snugly** over underwear only.

But I'm Between Sizes!

If you are be-
tween sizes, **select the small size**. Pattern companies add enough ease to cover you until you get to the next size.

Size	6	8	10	12	14	16	18	20	22	24
Bust	30½	31½	32½	34	36	38	40	42	44	46
Waist	23	24	25	26½	28	30	32	34	37	39
Hip	32½	33½	34½	36	38	40	42	44	46	48
Back Waist Length	15½	15¾	16	16¼	16½	16¾	17	17¼	17⅜	17½

For example, if you measure 33¾" in the full bust, sew with a size 10. A 12 probably would be too large in the neck and shoulders.

> **NOTE:** Ninety percent of the time, we successfully select a size for our students using only the high bust measurement in place of the bust measurement. Using the measurement you took for high bust, find that measurement on the "bust" line of the pattern size chart.

But My Top and Bottom are Different Sizes

Seventy percent of the people who sew are one size on top and another on the bottom. When buying coordinates, buy the pattern to fit your top. The top is much harder to alter. It is easy to make the bottom smaller or larger.

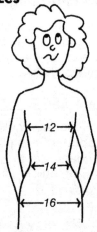

When buying a "bottoms only" pattern, go by your hip measurement. You can always take in or let out the waist. The exception is with full skirts and **very** full pants, if your waist is very small. Purchase those patterns by your waist measurement.

But the Pattern Doesn't Come in My Size!

People who are tall, petite, large or small always ask, "Why do the pattern companies ignore us?" They don't! However, if every pattern came in sizes 6 through 24, stores wouldn't have the space to hold them all. Therefore, pattern companies have had to find some **creative solutions**.

Some companies are printing 3 sizes on one tissue. Some are printing "petitable" adjustment lines on misses-sized patterns. One company is using a large-size person to select patterns for their large-size section. Quality, not quantity, is an excellent solution!

But what if you are a size 4 and don't want to sew teen patterns, or a size 18 and you've fallen in love with a design that goes only to a size 16?

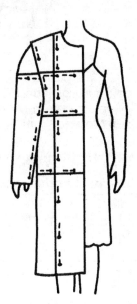

Actual pattern grading is tedious and complicated. However, you can get a similar results by simply tucking or spreading a pattern in the places shown. Then **try on the tissue** to see if you have tucked or spread in the right places. (See page 62.)

NOTE: Tuck or spread the front and back pattern pieces the same amount so they can be sewn together. Also, if you adjust the upper chest area, adjust the sleeve cap the same amount.

Understanding Ease

The difference between the size of your garment and the size of your body is called "ease." Pattern companies automatically add ease to body measurements. There are **three** types of ease allowed in patterns.

Comfort Ease

This is the **minimum** amount of ease pattern companies allow for "wiggle room" or room to move, sit, and walk comfortably.

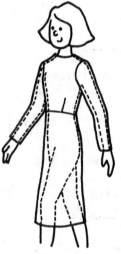

Design Ease

This is the amount of fullness added to a garment in addition to comfort ease to give it the look intended by the designer.

No Ease

Some patterns have little or no ease. Sometimes it's because of a look, such as jeans. Other times it is a pattern for a stretchy fabric. Swimsuits even have **minus ease**. If they don't "stretch to fit," you might lose the suit.

Ease Varies with...
Size and Body Type   *AND*   Garment Type

Min. ease in:	Misses	Half-Size	Women's
Bust	2½"	3½"	3½"
Waist	1"	1"	1"
Hip	2½"	2½"	2¾"

	Bust	Hip
Fitted Dress	4–8	3–5
Loose Blouse	10–15	8–10
Jacket	8–10	8–10
Oversized Coat	15+	15+

Finished Garment Measurements—
Your Clue to Design Ease

The best guides to the amount of ease in a design are the description on the back of the pattern envelope, the line drawings, and actual finished garment measurements. McCall's now prints these on the back of the pattern envelope.

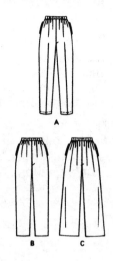

FINISHED GARMENT MEASUREMENTS									
Back length from natural waistline									
Pants A	40	40¼	40½	40¾	41	41¼	41½	41¾	Ins.
Pants B, C	41	41¼	41½	41¾	42	42¼	42½	41¾	"
Measurement at hipline									
Pants A, B	43½	45	47	49	51	53	55	57	"
Pants C	46	47½	49½	51½	53½	55½	57½	59½	"
Width, each leg									
Pants A	13	13½	14	14½	15	15½	16	16½	"
Pants B	17½	18	18½	19	19½	20	20½	21	"
Pants C	26½	27	27½	28	28½	29	29½	30	"

Ease is Personal Preference

Some people **like** tight clothes and others like loose-fitting clothes. The amount of ease that **you** find comfortable is personal preference. It varies with size, age, and lifestyle.

The "Pinch Test"

To find out the **minimum** amount of ease **you** prefer in fitted garments, try on various jackets, blouses, straight skirts and pants in your wardrobe and **pinch** them.

In a skirt, pull all the excess fabric to one side at the hip. If you can pinch ½", that is 1" ease; are you comfortable? If so, make all straight skirts that much larger than your body.

If you are still not sure about the **minimum** amount of ease to allow in a fitted design, we recommend the following for comfort if you are a size 12. If you are smaller or larger, you can subtract or add a little.

Bust	2½" - 3"
Hip	2" - 3"
Waist	1" - 1½"
Upper Arm	1½" - 3"

Tissue Fitting

Tissue fitting prevents sewing disasters! It helps you determine the amount of ease in the design and it also helps you visualize the silhouette on your body. Are the proportions good? Is there too much fullness? Would gathers be better than darts? One thing we have found, if the design doesn't look good in tissue, a $100-a-yard silk isn't going to make it look better!

Trim around the pattern tissue and press it with a warm dry iron. Pin seamlines of all pieces together. Pin in sleeves **after** fitting shoulder area. Clip fitted neckline and armhole seams so you won't tear the pattern. Now — try on the tissue! Pin the pattern to your center front and back — to your underwear, that is! If tissue fitting a jacket, try it on over a blouse.

Check the following:	**Then pin in sleeve and check it.**

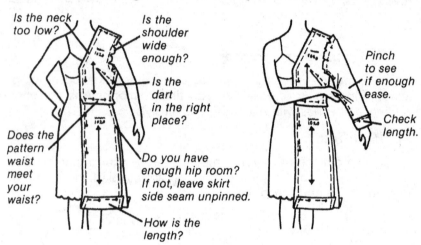

Is the neck too low?

Is the shoulder wide enough?

Is the dart in the right place?

Does the pattern waist meet your waist?

Do you have enough hip room? If not, leave skirt side seam unpinned.

How is the length?

Pinch to see if enough ease.

Check length.

Sway back or erect back

If your side seams swing forward, or the hem touches your legs at the center back, you either have a sway or an erect back. This **must** be caught **before** cutting. Shorten the center back by taking a tuck somewhere between the armhole and waist until pattern center back hangs straight. Straighten center back and grainline by drawing lines connecting top and bottom.

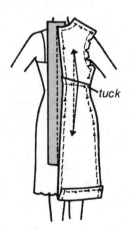

tuck

Pattern Companies are Standardized

The pattern companies know that you can't try on a pattern before you buy it to check the fit. Therefore, they have standardized their sizing. You will note that the bust measurement in the fitting chart is the same for all **major** companies.

Don't use ready-to-wear as a guide to your size. The only size standards manufacturers follow is "the more you pay, the smaller the size you can be." Pati's size 14 derriere got into a size 8 Anne Klein pant that sold for $600. She almost bought them! We call this **vanity sizing**! However, when Susan fit into a size 0 she wasn't necessarily flattered.

Ready-to-wear manufacturers don't have standards, because you can try on the merchandise before you buy it. Some ready-to-wear manufacturers design for a young audience and some for a mature audience. Have you noticed how some skirts fit you better in the waistline than others?

All pattern companies use a "sloper" or master pattern as the basis for all designs. We have actually overlaid their slopers and they are virtually identical. However, even though all major pattern company slopers are similar in shape, the amount of ease added to the design varies with fashion trends. See page 60 for more on **ease**.

Also, the pattern companies use a 20-year-old as their fit model. It makes sense when you stop to think about it. As we mature, our bodies change differently — remember genetics and gravity? If they fit to a young firm shape and stick to the standards, we can always make adjustments as we change.

Most of the companies have a **basic fitting pattern** with instructions to help you find out how your body is different from the "standard." It is a darted bodice with set-in sleeves and a fitted skirt. It has minimum ease.

The fitted style really shows off your shape. Make it in ¼" woven gingham and the built-in grainline will show up your "figure variations" even more! (Remember, they are not **problems**, just variations!)

Once you fit yourself and find out you have sloping shoulders or broad shoulders or a thick waist, you can make the same alterations whether you sew a McCall's or a Vogue. Sloping shoulders won't go away just because you switch from a Butterick to a Simplicity.

Why Use Gingham?

- Built-in grainline makes fitting faster.

- The checks make pattern alterations easy. After you've adjusted the gingham, just count the ¼" checks and you'll know the size of the adjustments you'll need to make on the pattern.

- Gingham is lightweight and soft enough to imitate knits, yet also acts like a woven fabric because it is one.

Fit in the following order:

Fit the Bodice   **Fit the Sleeve**   **Fit the Skirt**   **Fit the Dress**

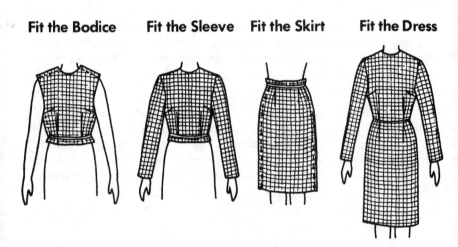

When the horizontal checks are parallel to the floor and the vertical checks are perpendicular to the floor and you have no wrinkles you have a "perfect" fit.

Take Time Now to Save Time Later

If all of this intimidates you, take a fitting class. The help of a teacher or a friend is invaluable. Someone else can look at you more impartially. A trained eye can more quickly spot figure variations. We get a lot of "aha's" in our seminars and workshops when we spot the reason for poor fit on a student and then offer a solution.

Make a Body Graph

We've just discussed making a sloper to analyze your body shape. Another tool is a "body graph." This is a quick, fun and simple way to identify your shape and proportions regardless of your height.

1. Cut newsprint or Perfect Pattern Paper wider and taller than you are. Fold it in half lengthwise and crease. Mark the foldline using a pen and a yardstick.

2. In an uncarpeted room, tape the paper to a wall. Cut or crease the paper even with the floor.

3. Stand with your back against the paper in normal posture, centering your body along the vertical crease. Have a friend mark the top of your head and crotch first to make sure you are centered on the fold. Look straight ahead. DO NOT LOOK UP OR DOWN!

4. Plot the points shown in the illustration below, using a new, long pencil, and a nonflexing yardstick.

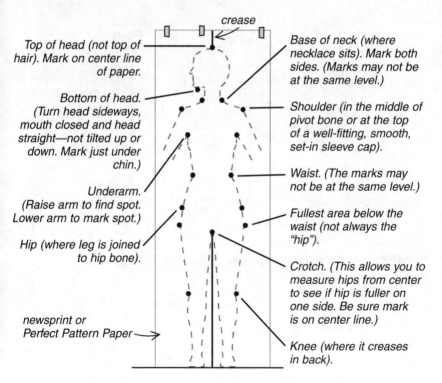

crease

Top of head (not top of hair). Mark on center line of paper.

Bottom of head. (Turn head sideways, mouth closed and head straight—not tilted up or down. Mark just under chin.)

Underarm. (Raise arm to find spot. Lower arm to mark spot.)

Hip (where leg is joined to hip bone).

newsprint or Perfect Pattern Paper →

Base of neck (where necklace sits). Mark both sides. (Marks may not be at the same level.)

Shoulder (in the middle of pivot bone or at the top of a well-fitting, smooth, set-in sleeve cap).

Waist. (The marks may not be at the same level.)

Fullest area below the waist (not always the "hip").

Crotch. (This allows you to measure hips from center to see if hip is fuller on one side. Be sure mark is on center line.)

Knee (where it creases in back).

For more in-depth information, see *Looking Good and Fit For Real People* (see page 127 of this book).

Two Ways to Alter Patterns

All alteration methods fall into two categories:

1. Cut into the tissue by...

altering where
it is needed
and filling in
with tissue,

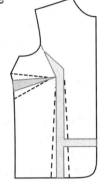

OR
by moving
seam
allowances
and filling in
with tissue.

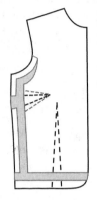

2. Add to outside edges by...
adding tissue AND tissue fitting,

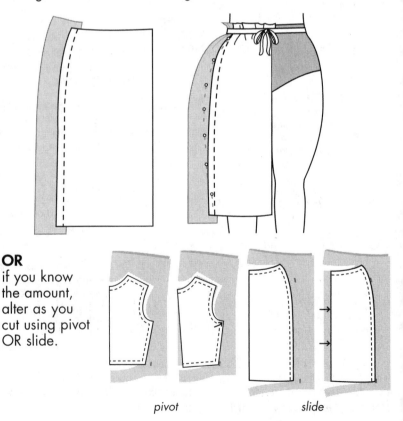

OR
if you know
the amount,
alter as you
cut using pivot
OR slide.

pivot   slide

Which Method to Use?

When we just need a little more waist or hip width or a more square shoulder, we generally add tissue to the outside edge of the pattern pieces. Then we try on the tissue and put pins in where we want the seam line to be. That way we can pin to fit our exact curves.

There are alterations we make most of the time by cutting into the tissue. These include full bust, full arms and round back. Cutting into the pattern puts the extra length and width exactly where you need it.

We use the pivot or slide methods less than we used to because they don't allow you to try on the tissue and check the fit before you cut. However, to change the length of an A-line skirt, the slide method is great because of the curved lower edge.

Use the Slide Method to Lengthen or Shorten an A-line Skirt

1. Determine how much length you want to add.

| 2. Chalk mark the new length. | 3. Cut all but the hem area. | 4. Slide the pattern to the marks and continue cutting across the lower edge. |

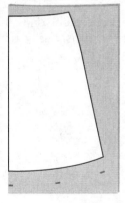 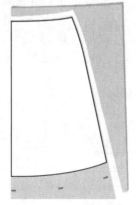 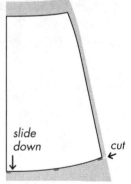

slide down ↓   *cut* ←

To make the A-line skirt shorter, mark above the hemline and raise the pattern before cutting the hem.

Professional Alteration Tips and Tools

Form neat alteration habits regardless of which way you decide to alter patterns, pivot and slide or slash and spread.

- First trim around the tissue OUTSIDE the black line to improve your accuracy when cutting fabric. It keeps the tissue from moving during the cutting process. Also, if using a multi-sized pattern, pre-trimming on the correct lines helps prevent mistakes.

- Do not tissue fit or cut using wrinkled tissue!! Press it with a DRY IRON set at the wool setting. A "warm" iron isn't hot enough. Steam and water drips spoil the pattern tissue. Empty water from the iron if dripping is a problem.

- You need a large work surface. No part of your tissue should hang off the surface while altering. The surface must be pinnable. Cardboard is the easiest surface on which to work.

  Buy a gridded folding cardboard cutting board or a gridded cardboard cutting table. The grid makes altering easier.

- Always put tape on the right side of the tissue and always press the wrong side of the tissue. Make this a habit! Alter with pattern pieces RIGHT SIDE up. Put alteration tissue UNDER the pattern. Tape pattern to alteration tissue from the RIGHT SIDE of the pattern. After taping, always press the WRONG side of the tissue only, so the iron won't directly touch the tape.

- Use Scotch® Magic® Transparent Tape®, the translucent one. It won't scrunch the tissue or buckle under the iron as easily as clear tape does. Use ½" tape as ¾" is too wide!

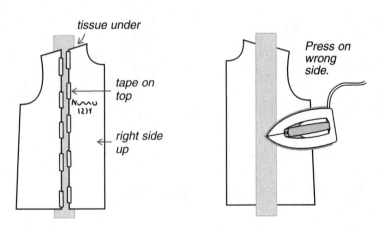

tissue under

tape on top

right side up

Press on wrong side.

- Use a pencil. We used to use a red, plastic-tip pen to mark alterations on the pattern, but it penetrates the tissue and makes a mess of your cutting board.

- Invest in 1⅜" extra fine (.5mm) glass head pins. These won't melt! Dritz, Collins, and Clotilde offer wonderful, quality pins.

- Strengthen the tissue of fitted patterns by taping the neckline and armhole curves, just inside the seamline with tissue right side up. Lap short pieces of tape ½" around the curves.

  In curved areas, clip through the seam allowance up to, but not through the tape.

  Tug lightly on tissue to see if it is taped securely.

- Pin, pin, and pin!

1. Place alteration tissue under the area to be altered. Anchor the parts of the pattern that won't be moved when making the desired alteration.

2. Anchor the alteration tissue.

3. Alter and anchor the parts you have moved.

4. Now, tape in place and trim away excess tissue.

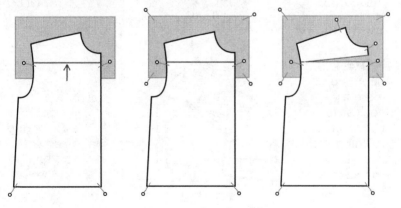

Do not tape as you go. Tape **only** after all pieces are pinned and lying totally flat.

Fit Glossary of Common Problems

NOTE: For the most complete guide to fit see our book **Fit for REAL People** (page 127).

Full Bust

Patterns are designed for the average B bra cup size. The C cup figure may have no problem in most styles, but a D or DD cup may need more room in most styles. A gaping front armhole and pulls across the bustline mean you need this alteration.

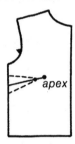 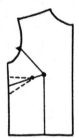 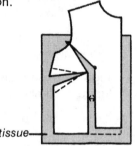

tissue⏤

1. Draw a line through dart to point of bust (apex). If pattern does not have a dart, pick a place you'd like to have one.

2. Draw a line from waist to apex parallel to grain and then to arm-hole notch.

3. Cut along lines to, but not through, arm-hole. At arrow, spread a mini-mum of:
   ½" for C cup
   ¾" for D cup
   1¼"+ for DD cup

4. Even up lower front edge.

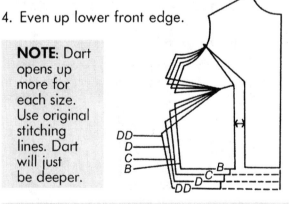

NOTE: Dart opens up more for each size. Use original stitching lines. Dart will just be deeper.

NOTE: Take in side front seam or add a vertical dart here if too large in waist.

NOTE: Three bonuses of this alteration...your armhole will no longer gape; you will have more width across the bust; you will have more length going over your fuller bust and your garments will no longer hike up at bottom in the front.

When a Pattern Has No Dart

Many patterns do not have darts. Even though extra ease may have been added, they may need more shaping to fit a D or DD.

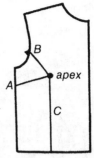

1. Find apex — Try pattern on and mark point of bust with a soft tip pen.

2. Draw line (A) on your pattern where you would like a dart.

3. Draw line (B) from apex to armhole notch.

4. Draw line (C) vertically below apex to bottom.

5. Cut and spread amount needed. Insert tissue. Opening becomes dart.

6. Draw dart to point to your apex.

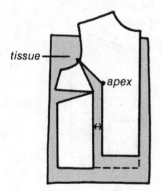

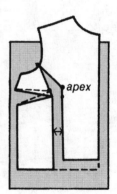

An Alternative to the Full Bust Alteration

If you are full in both the chest and upper arm and just need a little extra fullness, try the following. Add same amount to sleeve and bodice front and back. Taper in 6-8" down unless full in arms and waist, then taper further down.

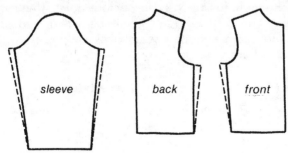

How to Move a Dart

You may need to raise, lower, shorten or lengthen darts until they point to the bust point (apex), but stop ½"- 1" from point. Pin pattern pieces together, then...

Try on the tissue. Mark **your** bust point with soft tip pen.

To raise dart, redraw higher.

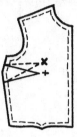

To lower dart, redraw lower.

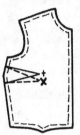

Or, draw a box around each dart and cut out the box.

Move darts until they point to your apex.

To Shorten a Dart

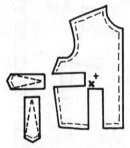

To Lengthen a Dart

NOTE: A well-stitched dart will fit better! Shorten stitches to 1.5mm stitch length for the last 1½" before point. The last ¼"-½" should be right on edge of fabric. Chain off. Pull dart towards you and stitch the chain into dart seam allowance. Sew a "curved dart" for curved areas.

regular dart

curved dart

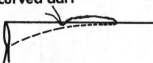

Broad Shoulders

Pivot the pattern out.

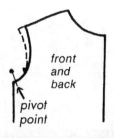

front
and
back

pivot
point

Narrow Shoulders

Pivot the pattern in and cut narrower.

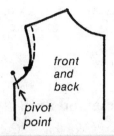

front
and
back

pivot
point

NOTE: See page 69 for square and sloping shoulder adjustments.

Wide Back

Spread pattern in shoulder area. Add a shoulder dart or ease, or sew the back armhole seam deeper until back shoulder fits front.

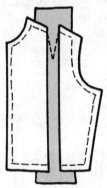

Narrow Back

Tuck back through shoulder area. Let out back armhole seam until back shoulder fits front. (Or, if there is a shoulder dart, sew it narrower.)

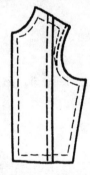

NOTE: Straighten ("true") seamlines as shown when necessary.

Sway Back, Erect Back, or Flat Derriere

If skirts and dresses normally hang longer in back or your side seams swing forward, take a tuck in the pattern at center back as shown on page 62. For skirts and pants, lower waistband when fitting as you sew as shown on page 77.

Slightly Rounded Back

Make shoulder dart deeper until gap in armhole disappears. Let out back armhole seam until back matches front. (See our *Fit* book for more alternatives.)

Very Rounded Back

Often looks like this in a garment. Center back is not long enough and armhole gaps.

Cut pattern on these lines.

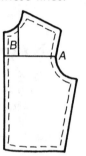

Spread across back (A) until neckline is raised enough to meet yours. Spread (B) until center back is straight. Make (B) into a neck dart 2-3" long so neck isn't enlarged.

Sleeve too tight in upper arm

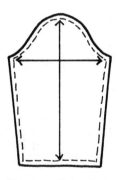

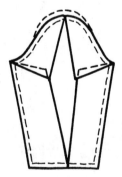

Draw a line down center of sleeve parallel to grain and across from underarm to underarm seam.

Cut on these lines and spread desired amount. If more than 1", redraw original cap.

Spread a two-piece sleeve as shown above.

Fit-As-You-Sew

This is the key to perfection! Try on your garment **during EACH STEP of construction** before a full-length mirror. See how it looks, feels, and hangs. (Smile and comb your hair...the garment will look better, even if it's not finished!)

Keep in Mind These Two Points Before Beginning:

1. The bigger the **body bumps**, the more length, width, and deeper darts they will need.

NOTE: Pati used to think that people with small busts needed to take deeper darts to get rid of all that extra fullness. She finally realized that men don't have darts! If you are flat-chested, you need narrower darts and less length and width over the bustline.

2. Sew the same curves in the side seams of your garment that you have on your body. If you don't have any, then you'd better straighten up that side seam!

How to Fit-As-You-Sew

1. Cut pattern, making necessary adjustments.

2. Mark darts.

3. Staystitch (important since you will be fitting).

4. Sew darts and all seams but side and shoulder seams.

5. Pin-baste remaining seams **wrong sides together**.

6. Try on **right side out** since right and left sides of body may be different. (Have ¼" elastic tied around your waist to mark it. The **bottom** of the elastic is your waist.)

7. Fit.

8. After you have marked all of your adjustments, mark new seamlines. Spread open seam allowances and mark at pins on wrong side of fabric using tailors' chalk or water-soluble marker.

What to Look For When Fitting-As-You-Sew

Fit from the top down or where your garment hangs from your body. Check the following:

- Are the shoulder seams in the center of the shoulder?
- Is shoulder width correct?
- Are darts pointing to bust, yet ending ½"-1" from apex?
- Are the side seams hanging straight?
- Is the garment too tight or too loose?
- Do you have any wrinkles? They usually point to the problem.

Adjusting on the Body is Easy

Make the following adjustments right on the body. A skirt will be illustrated, but the adjustments relate to pants or dresses as well.

1. Horizontal wrinkles mean skirt is too tight. Let out side seams.

2. Vertical wrinkles mean it is too loose. Take in side seams.

3. Hip is high and full on one side.

Pull up on low side. (Or, you could pull down on high side.)

4. Flat derriere and/or full tummy.

Pull up in back and down in front until side seam is straight.

Mother Pletsch's Truths

PODIUM

There are some things in sewing that are just plain **"TRUTHS"** — like the sun rises in the east and sets in the west. We can argue and fiddle with new and different ways of sewing, but a few **truths** remain.

Truth # 1

Grainline — the direction of threads in a woven fabric. Generally the lengthwise grain is the strongest, the crosswise is slightly stretchy, and the bias is very stretchy.

To find **true bias** in wovens, fold the fabric until the lengthwise grain is parallel to the crosswise grain. The fold line is the "true bias."

How to Straighten Off-Grain Fabrics

If your fabric isn't square when you cut, your clothes won't hang properly. To straighten off-grain fabrics, tear or pull a thread and cut along the crosswise grainline.

Then straighten or "square" the grain. Place the fabric on a table with square corners.

If the fabric doesn't follow the lines of the table, pull on the short ends until it does.

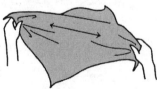

Another method is to square the fabric by steaming it. Pin fabric to a pressing table (some people use their beds). Steam. After cooling and drying, the fabric should remain square.

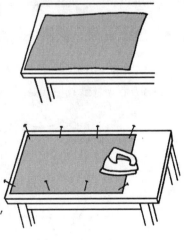

NOTE: Some permanent-press fabrics are "permanently off-grain." Avoid prints, stripes and plaids that are printed off-grain.

Truth # 2

Staystitching — stitch ½" from the edge next to stitching line within seam allowance. It doesn't have to be painful, and sometimes just can't be avoided. The **two** times it is important to staystitch are:

1. **When fitting** — to prevent edges from stretching.
2. **When the edge is to be clipped** — for strength. For example, staystitch a neckline before clipping to apply a collar.

Fabrics that most need staystitching — loosely woven and ravelly fabrics; fabrics made from natural fibers; and interlock knits (on the edge that runs). We generally do not staystitch lightweight single knits or silkies. It makes the edges draw up and pucker.

Directional staystitching — means to staystitch in the direction of the grain. If you staystitch against the grain, you may stretch the edge just by stitching on it. How do you know which direction to staystitch? There are **two** rules:

1. Staystitch in the direction of the threads...

(It's like stroking a kitty. Staystitch "with the fur," not against it.)

2. Staystitch from wide to narrow.

   As a general rule, use these directions for a bodice and a skirt.

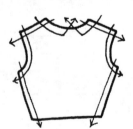 

> **NOTE**: When staystitching neck, pivot and sew off fabric edge. It makes snipping off those threads easier and also allows you to use the "continuous stitching" technique.

Truth # 3

Continuous staystitching — is a time and thread saver. Use a regular stitch length (2.5mm) and stitch ½" from the edge. Just feed one piece after another into the machine and step on the accelerator and GO! See, staystitching doesn't have to be painful!

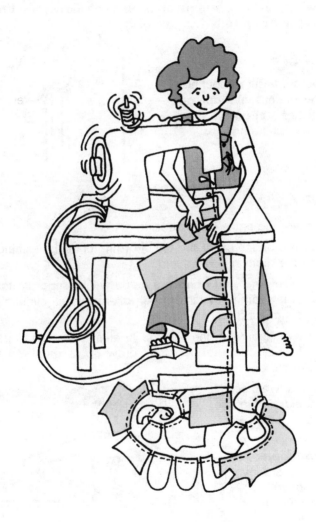

Truth # 4

Sometimes the things that seem like extra work are really time-savers in the end — like pressing a tissue pattern before cutting. It makes cutting faster and more accurate.

Truth # 5

Do what you hate the most or think will be the hardest **first**. Then the rest is psychologically super easy!

Truth # 6

If you are unsure about how two pieces of unusual shape are sewn together, **get out your pattern**. Match the notches and dots.

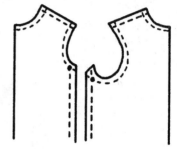

Truth # 7

There **are** ways to make cutting easier:

1. If a seam is on the exact straight of grain, it may be eliminated by placing the seamline on the fold.

2. Many jacket and shirt fronts are made with a separate facing. If the grain is straight, match up the pattern pieces, eliminating the seam, to make it a "cut-on" facing.

3. Cut straight seams on the selvage to eliminate seam finishing in woven fabrics. New fabrics don't draw up or shrink on the selvage like old ones did.

4. Change a two-piece rectangular cuff to one.

5. How to avoid cutting frustration — **buy enough fabric**. Computerized layouts make pattern companies much more accurate in yardage calculations.

Truth # 8

Reducing bulk is one of the most important of our truths. A bulky enclosed seam can make a garment look very tacky. Before turning a collar, a pocket, or a faced neckline to the inside, try these ways to reduce bulk:

1. Trim seams to ¼".

2. Grade or "layer" one seam to ⅛".

NOTE: A speedy way to trim and grade in one step is to "bevel." Slant your scissors until 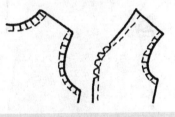 they are almost flat over the seam and trim. This automatically makes the top layer shorter.

3. Clip inward curves.

4. Notch outward curves.

NOTE: For easy notching, use pinking shears. Or, use very small stitches so you can trim close and eliminate notching.

NOTE: To prevent raveling, use small stitches whenever trimming, grading, notching, or clipping close to a seamline.

Truth # 9

To further flatten an enclosed seam, **understitch**. This means to stitch the seam allowances to the facing. It is used mainly on necklines, collars and armholes. Use a regular stitch length and stitch ⅛" from well of seam. Use one of the following stitch types.

1. Straight stitch.

2. Blind hemming stitch.

Pretty
Pati's
Pointers

Pati always remembers things best when she knows the logic behind the concept — so she teaches sewing in that way. Pati's pointers are basic ideas in sewing that apply to most sewing tasks, and they are ideas that make sewing so-o-o-o-o much easier. Many sewing books touch on these thoughts, but we want to emphasize them!

Pointer # 1

How do you sew two edges together that are **completely different in shape?**

Straight collar

Curved neckline

1. Staystitch ½" from edge.

2. Clip to staystitching.

3. Spread neckline.

4. Pin collar in place.

5. Sew to neck edge.

Pointer # 2

How to "key" facings to necklines, armholes, or tops of skirts or pants to make them lie flat. (The ugliest thing is a facing that doesn't **fit** and shows on the outside!)

1. Lay front facing in place. Smooth flat and pin.
2. Where facing overlaps seamline, snip.

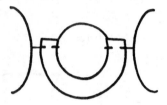

3. Fold front away from shoulder. Pin the back facing in place and snip where back falls over seam.

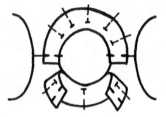

4. With facing ends right sides together, line up snips and stitch.

5. Trim facing seam to ¼" and press open.

6. Match seamlines of facing and garment with pins through both seamlines.

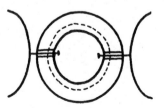

7. Stitch, trim, grade, understitch, turn, and press.

Pointer # 3

Use a **slipstitch** to fasten two layers together **invisibly**. Stitch through one "tunnel," **straight down** to second "tunnel," **straight up** to first tunnel etc. Pull threads tight until they disappear! Use on...

Pockets

NOTE: Fold garment back to create two tunnels. It's easier!

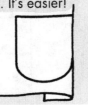

Hand rolled hems, continuous plackets.

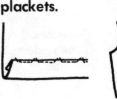

Linings

Pointer # 4

Stitching in the well of the seam has 100 uses. One of our favorite uses is for a waistband.

Topstitch from outside **in well of seam**. This catches the band on underside. The **shorter the stitch, the more invisible it is**.

NOTE: Cut inside edge of woven waistbands on selvage or finish with zigzagging or serging.

Other uses:
Quickie cuff

Stand up collars

Tacking facings down

Quickie self-binding on knit tops

In seams to keep elastic from rolling

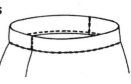

Pointer # 5

An inside circle, like an inner cylinder, must be smaller. Wherever two layers of fabric go around your body together, make the inside layer smaller. This allows for what is termed "turn of cloth."

At the end of a waistband or cuff, trim ⅛" off the underside to nothing at fold line.

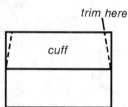

Make sure the edges meet when you sew the ends together.

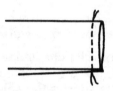

A collar also has "turn of cloth." The upper collar rolls over the undercollar creating an inner cylinder.

Trim ⅛" off (¼" for very heavy fabrics) from center front to center front. If collar points are acutely angled, trim little or nothing off at points or you won't be able to sew them together.

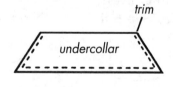

Match edges of upper collar and undercollar when you sew them together. This creates a "bubble" in upper collar that will disappear when collar is completed.

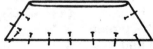

Pointer # 6

Ways to Topstitch Straight/Simplify Topstitching

- **Know your presser foot.** Measure the distance from the needle to the outside edge of the foot and the inside of the "toe." Most topstitching is done ¼" from the fabric edge and most edge stitching is ⅛" away, so the presser foot edges often can be used as guides. If your foot measures differently, change the standard and use what your foot measures as your topstitching guide. Or, move the needle position, if possible, to get the exact topstitching width you want.

- **Use the seam markings on the throat plate** for wider widths. For even wider widths not marked on your machine, apply masking tape and mark it off for easy-to-see stitching lines. If your machine does not have marking to the left of the foot, put tape on that side also, because sometimes it is better to sew with the fabric to the right. If necessary, put another tape strip in front of the foot ⅝" from the needle to help you pivot around a corner.

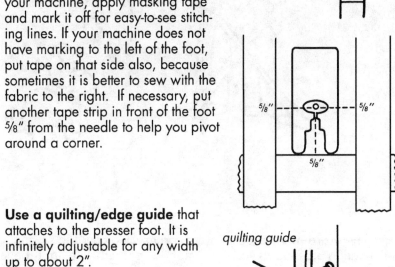

throat plate guide

- **Use a quilting/edge guide** that attaches to the presser foot. It is infinitely adjustable for any width up to about 2".

quilting guide

- **Use topstitching tape** for accurate stitching within the garment.

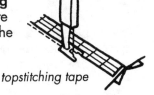

topstitching tape

Press As You Sew

There are many places to cut corners and cheat in sewing, but eliminating pressing as you sew is not one of them. We firmly believe that even some so-called "sewing disasters" can be made wearable by good pressing techniques. Good pressing can hide a multitude of sins!

Pressing is another one of the places where the right tools for the task are a necessity. Susan sews a great deal during her travels and yet wherever she travels her suitcase of pressing aids follows. She swears she can't sew without them!

The Necessities

1. **Pressing ham (tailor's ham)** — a ham-shaped surface ideal for pressing curved and shaped areas. Helps give "people shape" to flat fabric.

2. **Seam roll** — a sausage-shaped aid used to press open flat seams. Great for cylinders like sleeves and pant legs. The seam allowances fall over the edge of the roll and allow your iron to touch only the stitching line itself.

3. **Point presser/clapper** — a wooden combination tool. The point presser is used to press open seams and points, and the clapper forces steam into fabric to help flatten it. The wood helps form sharp creases as its cool surface draws the heat and steam out of the pressed fabric. (When still warm, fabrics spring back to their unpressed state; they have a "memory" only when cooled.)

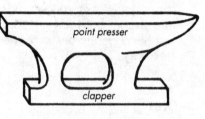

point presser

clapper

4. **"Shot-of-steam" type iron** — a super steaming iron with an extra button to press for a jet of steam that will press even the most stubborn fabric. A non-stick coating is great. Many sewers prefer irons without automatic shut-off.

5. **See-through press cloth** — sheer cloth that allows you to see what you're pressing.

You need not purchase all of these items at one time. Remember that these pieces are a lifetime investment in quality sewing. Budget to regularly buy additional tools, or put them on your Christmas or birthday wish list.

How to Press

A Seam

1. Press flat first to remove any puckers.

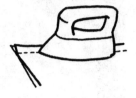

2. Place open over seam roll. Press.

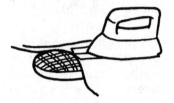

3. Place point presser/clapper on top of seam and apply light pressure. The clapper used to be called a pounding block because fabrics were actually pounded into shape, but today's fabrics just need gentle pressure, **not a beating**.

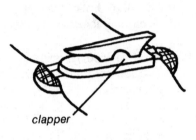

clapper

A Dart

Press flat first to crease the fold line and to remove any puckers. Place the dart over the appropriate curve of the ham and tuck clean paper under fold to prevent an indentation from showing on the right side.

> **NOTE**: There is a curve on every ham to fit the shape of any body curve. Bust darts go over a very round curve and skirt darts over a flatter one.

NOTE: If dart is bulky, clip open. Before pressing, put strips of paper under edges as shown, to prevent press marks on right side.

A Finished Edge
with Enclosed Seams

This applies to collar, jacket front, and curved neckline edges. Press open over seam roll, ham, or point presser, whichever is the best fit.

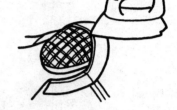

Turn right side out. Roll the seam slightly toward the inside to prevent it from showing. Final press. (Place curved edges over a ham.) **To crease edge**, press firmly with a clapper until fabric cools.

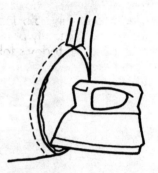

A Set-in Sleeve

Always press the seam allowance from inside the sleeve.

Pressing Tips

1. **Press with an "up and down" motion** of the iron whenever possible. Sliding the iron can cause stretching and shine.

2. **Vertical darts** are pressed toward the center for consistency.

3. **Horizontal darts** are pressed up. We're not just trying to be different. We think this gives a smoother, higher-busted younger look.

4. **Fingers are a FREE pressing tool!** You can finger press a seam or dart in the right direction **before** pressing with the iron.

5. **Pressing takes PATIENCE!** Don't move the fabric until it completely cools or you'll put wrinkles back into what you just pressed. Fabrics have a memory **only** when cool!

6. **Press lightly.** Heavy pressing can cause an overpressed, shiny, "I'm old and worn" look in a new fabric. Synthetic fabrics are more heat sensitive than natural fabrics, so use a very light touch with these.

7. **If top-pressing** is necessary, test iron on a scrap of fabric to see if **a press cloth** is necessary.

Necessary Details

"Having trouble with sleeves and cuffs?"

Sleeves

The term set-in sleeve can bring tears to the eyes of even the hardiest home sewer — yet it doesn't have to. There are many tricks that can make any sleeve a snap to sew. For example, the following **work order** seems to be easiest in achieving a professional-looking cuffed sleeve:

1. Complete placket.*
2. Complete cuff.
3. Sew cuff to sleeve.
4. Set sleeve into armhole.

*EXCEPTION: Complete placket after #3 if using "Marta's Painless Placket," page 97.

We will give you several methods for completing each step. Why not try them all and find the one you like best. Some of the "quickie" methods are not always best, because they may not look good if you turn back your cuffs.

We will attack one part of the sleeve at a time in the order they are "usually" completed: placket, cuff, and sleeve.

Sleeve Openings — Formerly Called Plackets (Ugh!)

With the exception of Pati, consensus ruled that the traditional continuous placket is a **pain**! Patterns are, however, doing a better job of illustrating how to sew them. If you want an alternative, here are some options.

Faced Placket

1. Cut sleeve and snip mark location of placket.

2. For each sleeve, cut one 2" X 3" bias rectangle of matching fabric. Use your fashion fabric, matching lining or fusible knit interfacing. (For how to find bias, see page 79.)

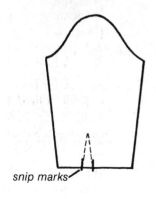

snip marks

3. Right sides
   together,
   center
   rectangle
   over snips.

4. Stitch a "V"
   2" long. Use
   tiny stitches
   at point.

5. Slash
   to point,
   turn, and
   press.

 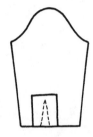 

To hold rectangle in place do one of the following:

From the right side, top-
stitch 1/8" - 1/4" from the
edge of the opening.

OR, cut a 1 1/2" X 2 1/2" patch of fusible
web with a center slit the length of the
opening. Place under facing. Fuse.

The "It's not cute — but it does the job fast" Placket

(This is not really a placket in the true sense, as there is no actual
opening.)

1. Snip center
   of placket
   opening
   and stay-
   stitch seam-
   line.

2. Clip to
   seamline
   on both
   sides of
   snip mark.

3. Fold 1"
   section twice
   to inside.
   Topstitch or
   slipstitch
   in place.

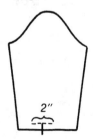  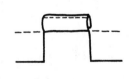

Marta's Painless Placket . . . the "When all else fails, turn the placket into a seam" Placket

Marta Alto, Palmer/Pletsch Associate and resident speed-sewing person, discovered this "in the seam" instant placket over 20 years ago...and made sewing dresses and blouses so much easier for us all.

It is easiest to sew on a straight sleeve, but works on fuller sleeves. Avoid it on shirt sleeves with flat caps — you need to be a designer to tackle them.

straight sleeve

full sleeve

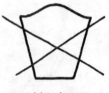

shirt sleeve

1. Draw a line through the center of the pattern placket markings parallel to the grain line.

2. Cut along that line.

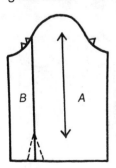

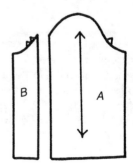

3. Reposition B so that the existing stitching lines overlap.

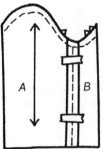

4. Add ⅝" seam allowances to **new** outside edges.

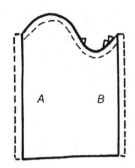

5. Cut sleeves.

NOTE: If the sleeve is straight, cut edge A on the selvage.

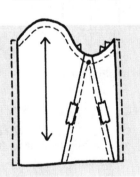

NOTE: If the sleeve isn't **completely** straight, overlap at underarm seam intersection. Then line up edges until parallel to grain line. Otherwise your new sleeve seam would have one bias and one straight edge.

If desired, you may add the fullness back in. However, a bias seam may not look as good in a plaid. Add **equally** to both sides of the sleeve. You may also want to cut it longer so it blouses over the cuff. Tissue fit to check length. (See page 62).

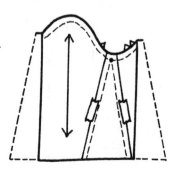

Cuffs are Easy with Marta's Painless Placket

1. Attach cuff while sleeve is flat! Trim undercuff ⅛" smaller on both sides, so it won't show when finished. Taper to nothing at fold. Press under ⅜" on long edge of undercuff.

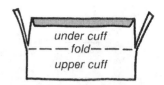

2. Fold under edge cut on selvage ⅝" and snip other edge ¼" and turn under. Turn under again ⅜".

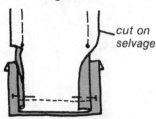

cut on selvage

NOTE: If neither edge was cut on selvage, snip seam allowance ¼" and turn under ¼" on both sides. Turn under again ⅜".

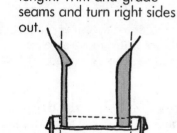

3. Sew cuff ends right sides together. Before stitching, make sure ends are same length. Trim and grade seams and turn right sides out.

4. "Stitch in the ditch" or well of seam from right side. You will catch cuff facing since you only pressed under ⅜".

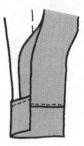

5. Sew sleeve seam.

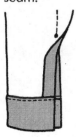

6. Press seam open over a seam roll.

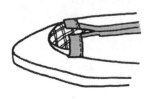

7. Topstitch placket in place.

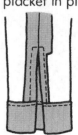

More Cuff Tips

You may stitch ends of cuff either before or after stitching it to sleeve.

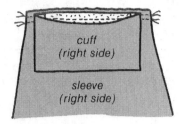 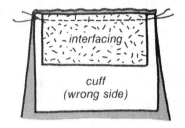

cuff
(right side)

sleeve
(right side)

interfacing

cuff
(wrong side)

You may wish to allow an
extension on the under cuff
side **or**...

you may sew
ends even with
placket edge.

 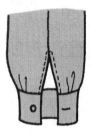

If in doubt, pin cuff to sleeve and try sleeve on your arm and overlap
where it would be buttoned. See how it looks. Just make sure placket
either overlaps or at least comes together so your skin doesn't show.

If you own a
serger, serge edges
of sleeve seam.

Fold edges over
cuff **tightly** and
machine baste.
Then serge the
seam. Knot thread
tails close to
sleeve seam.

Turn cuff down.
Stitch sleeve seam,
leaving placket
opening.

  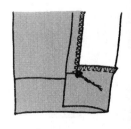

machine basting

Setting in a Sleeve

1. Easing the cap:

Susan's Method
Machine baste two rows of stitching from notch to notch over the sleeve cap. Place one row at ½" and the other at ¾" from the edge. Stitch between the two rows when setting in a sleeve.

Pati's Method
Machine baste two rows of stitching from notch to notch. Place one row at ⅜" and the other at ⅝" from the edge. Pull up on the ⅜" stitching line only. The ⅝" line is only a guide for your final stitching.

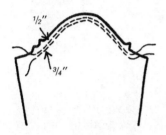

pull up on both threads

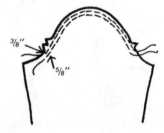

pull up on ⅜" thread only

NOTE: Place as little ease as possible in the top 2" of sleeve as it is on the straight of grain. This prevents puckering and pleating at the top.

2. Place sleeve in armhole, matching underarm seams, and pin. The second pin goes into the top of the sleeve, and the next two pins join the notches. Add any extra pins you need to make the ease even.

3. Machine baste sleeve in place.

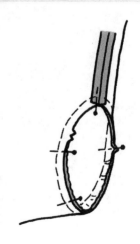

NOTE: The secret to any sleeve is knowing when and how to cheat! The time to do it is after machine basting. Before you do any final stitching on sleeve, check the outside to see if it is puckery. If it is, try one or more of the following CHEATS:

Smooth seam with your thumb and forefinger. Because the basting is loose, you can often smooth out any puckers!

If there are puckers, clip your basting and re-stitch. Sometimes, the second time is a charm!

Some bodies require more front or back sleeve fullness. The pattern gives you an average placement of fullness, so you must tailor this to your body's special needs depending on wrinkles you see.

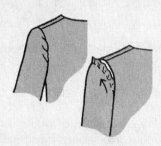

move fullness toward back   *move fullness toward front*

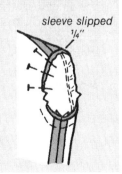

sleeve slipped 1/4"

When your sleeve cap puckers, remove basting. Slip sleeve cap ⅛" further into armhole. Machine baste again at garment ⅝" seam line. If cap still puckers, slip it another ⅛" . . . and another if necessary. When all else fails, place all the fullness at the very top and call it a gathered sleeve!

4. Final stitching:

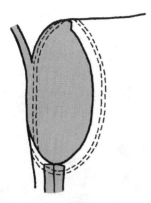

. . . Permanently stitch sleeve on ⅝" seamline. Stitch another row ¼" away.

. . . Trim to ¼" around armhole. In jackets trim from notch to notch at underarm keeping full ⅝" seam allowance at top of sleeve.

NOTE: The second row of stitching may be zig-zagging or serging.

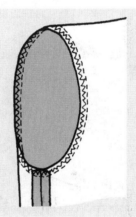

NOTE: For no more popped sleeve seams, use a stretch-overlock stitch. It is Pati's favorite. The one-step finish accomplishes the first and second row at the same time. Trim to ¼" after stitching. If you use the stretch-overlock stitch, your sleeve will NEVER rip out.

NOTE: For additional nifty ideas for setting in sleeves, see our books on Ultrasuede® and tailoring.

Other Set-In Sleeve Methods

Shirt-Type Sleeve — the Flat Method

The flat method is best on shirt-type sleeves with flat caps. For regular sleeves, fit is best when the underarm seam stands up under your arm.

1. Stitch shoulder seam of garment. Pin sleeve into armhole and stitch.

2. Stitch underarm seam of garment and sleeve.

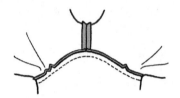 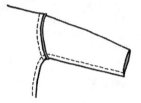

NOTE: Press seam open or to one side and topstitch for a "mock flat-felled" seam.

NOTE: This method does **not** work with "Marta's Painless Placket."

Modified Flat Method

This method incorporates the speed of the flat method, but can be used on conventional-type sleeves for a better fit. It is also excellent for the tiny armhole of a child's garment.

1. Stitch sleeve cap to garment from notch to notch **only**.

2. Stitch garment and sleeve underarm seams.

3. Complete stitching armhole seam from notch to notch under the arm.

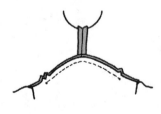 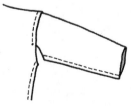 

Shoulder Pads

Shoulder pads are ideal for some bodies. A shoulder pad can turn sloping shoulders into normal without altering the clothing! Uneven shoulders can be made to match by using a thicker and a thinner pad. If shoulders are lumpy from deep bra strap marks, pads can smooth out the shoulders. Narrower shoulders can be widened with raglan pads to help balance heavier hips. The pad becomes your shoulder.

You can sew your own shoulder pads from our "No-Sew" instructions, or purchase ready-made ones. Before buying or making shoulder pads, be sure to note your fashion pattern's suggestion for shoulder pad shape and thickness.

Make shoulder pads the "No-Sew" way!

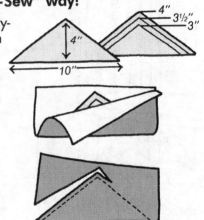

1. Cut one or more triangles of polyester fleece, and layer as shown for your desired thickness.

2. Place on fusible side of a 9" X 11" layer of fusible knit interfacing. Fuse all edges together.

3. Trim excess interfacing away to within ¼" of the fleece. Knit interfacings will not ravel, so finishing is unnecessary.

Covered Shoulder Pads

Covered shoulder pads are a nice touch in any better fabric garment, and help to camouflage the shoulder pad in a sleeveless garment.

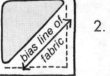

1. Place pad on wrong side of self fabric.

2. Stitch, then zigzag around pad or serge.

Attaching Shoulder Pads

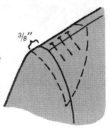

Try on the garment with shoulder pads pinned in place. **The edge of the pad should extend ⅜" into the sleeve**. Hand stitch to seam allowances.

Hems

A traditional hem can be beautiful. Follow these steps and your hem will never show on the outside:

1. Turn up desired hem (see next page for recommended widths). Press the crease lightly. **NEVER press over** the top edge of a hem. It may leave a permanent impression on the right side.

2. Grade seams in hem allowance to ¼".

3. Finish hem edge with one of the options shown on the next page.

4. If necessary, ease hem edge to fit skirt by machine basting ¼" from edge and pulling up on basting until hem fits.

5. Use the "designer hem stitch," our favorite because it NEVER shows.

   - Fold back the hem edge.
   - Use polyester thread. It **wears longer**!
   - Take long loose stitches catching only a **single fiber** of your outside fabric. (Use the smallest needle you can thread — a size 10 sharp is best!)
   - Every few stitches, pull or stretch hem horizontally to loosen stitches, and secure by knotting in hem allowance. This will protect the hem in case you accidently step into it.

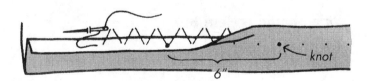

OR, use your machine blind hem stitch for a very sturdy hem — best for medium to heavy fabrics. It's great for children's wear and casual clothing.

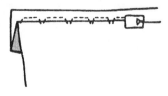

Hem Edge Finishes

The following finishes prevent raveling on woven fabrics. Knits don't need a finish unless they need stability such as an interlock knit that runs in one direction.

For fabrics that are hand washed, dry-cleaned, or lined, the following are least visible. They are also perfect for blouses you plan to tuck in. In fact, to eliminate bulk, we don't even turn up a hem.

Pink — less is best for lightweight wovens.

Stitch and pink for heavy cottons and wools.

The following are for fabrics that ravel and/or are machine washed:

Zigzag — for medium-weight fabrics.

Triple zigzag for lightweight fabrics that might bunch up with a zigzag.

Seams Great® or Seams Saver® for when you want a lightweight bound edge.

Serged — works on all fabrics to encase the edge.

How Wide Should a Hem Be?

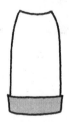

Straight skirt — 2-2½". (The wide hem helps it hang better.)

A-line skirt — 1½ -2". (The fuller the skirt the narrower the hem.)

Very full skirts — ¼" hand or machine rolled. Wider hems too hard to ease.

Other Hem Options

Decorative hems

Turn under the full hem and machine topstitch with a 4mm twin needle for a decorative effect.

Trim hem allowance to ½". Turn up ¼" twice. Press. Topstitch or topstitch **and** edgestitch.

Easy hems for full skirts

These hems are **great** for full skirts.

Trim hem allowance to 1/2". Turn up hem 1/4" and stitch close to fold. Turn up hem again 1/4". **Edgestitch** 1/16 - 1/8" from folded edge.

Serge the edge. Turn serging to wrong side. From right side, edgestitch 1/16 - 1/8" from fold.

Fused hems

Use a fused hem on double knits, children's, and work clothes. Test on a scrap of your fabric first to make sure the fusible web won't be too stiff. Cut web 1/4" narrower than hem width. Place next to fold. Turn up hem and fuse 10-15 seconds to within 1/4" of top edge.

The No-Hem Hem

Leave tuck-in blouses un-hemmed for the smoothest hipline. Pink or serge the edge. Press to make very flat.

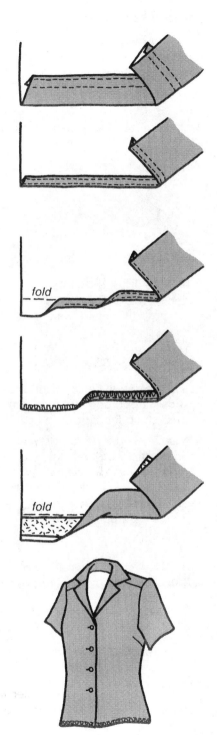

Zippers

If you buy a zipper 1-2" longer than you need, the slider won't get in your way and cause crooked topstitching. Sew in, then unzip the zipper, sew waistband or facing over top and cut off excess.

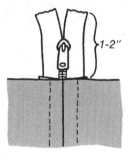

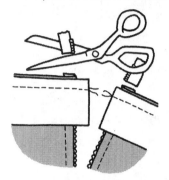

NOTE: Today's synthetic-coil zippers are self-locking. They don't need to be zipped to the top to stay up. This means they are now shortened from the top, not the bottom.

More Zipper Tips

- Put zippers in center front or back, even if the pattern calls for a side zipper, because then you can alter side seams without restitching the zipper.

- Use basting tape, a narrow tape that's sticky on both sides, to eliminate hand basting. It comes on a reel covered with protective paper. Stick it on edges of zipper, peel away paper, and stick zipper to fabric.

tape

NOTE: Do not stitch through basting tape. It will gum up your needle.

- Our favorite tip . . . find patterns with the no-zipper pocket opening. Then you'll have a truly painless zipper!

Centered Zipper

1. Permanently stitch seam to zipper opening. Backstitch. Machine baste seam closed. Break basting every 1-1½".

2. Press seam open. Place basting tape on right side of zipper edges. Center zipper coil over seam and stick in place.

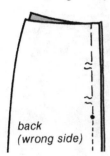

back
(wrong side)

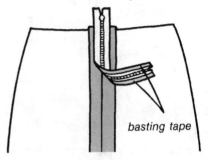

basting tape

3. Center ½" Scotch® brand Magic™ Tape over seam and topstitch along each side.

4. Remove basting tape. Remove Scotch tape and machine basting.

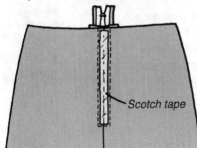

Scotch tape

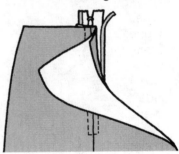

Lapped Zipper

1. Permanently stitch seam to zipper opening. Press under ½" on right side for **underlap** and ⅝" on left side for **overlap**.

2. Place basting tape on right edge of zipper. Stick zipper to underlap side and stitch from bottom to top close to teeth.

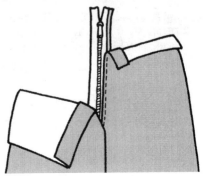

111

3. Place basting tape on **very edge** of overlap to keep it from slipping during topstitching.

basting tape

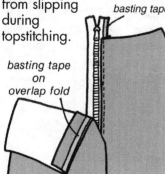

basting tape
on
overlap fold

4. Stick overlap in place. Place ½" Scotch™ brand Magic™ Tape next to edge of overlap. Pin through all layers. Topstitch next to tape.

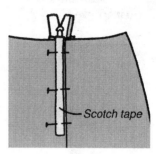

Scotch tape

Invisible Zippers Are Back'

The invisible zipper of the 70s was bulky. Today's has a fine coil. You can buy the special foot that opens the coil as you sew or use a zipper foot as follows:

Stitching is 1/2" from edge.

1. Open zipper. From the wrong side press the teeth flat so you can sew close to them.

2. Place open zipper right side down onto right side of fabric. You may use basting tape to hold zipper in place. The top edge of the zipper should match top of pant or skirt and the long edge should match edge of fabric. Sew next to teeth until front of foot hits the stopper.

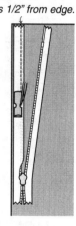

3. Sew other side the same way, as shown on the package.

4. Sew the rest of the seam. To avoid a pucker at the base of the zipper, start sewing ½" above and ⅛" out from the end of the zipper stitching (a ⅝" seam allowance).

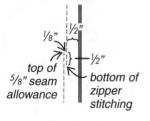

⅛"   ½"
½"
top of
⅝" seam
allowance

bottom of
zipper
stitching

Tip: With presser foot up and zipper standing on its side, lower needle into extact spot you want to start sewing. Do not backstitch. Lower the presser foot and stitch to the end of the seam. Pull threads through at beginning of seam and tie a knot.

Faced Necklines

Zippers are a common closure at the center back of dresses, but how do you finish the top of a faced neckline neatly? Try the following on faced waistlines too.

(For lapped zippers)

1. Fold edge of left facing back 1" and right facing ⅝", wrong sides together.

2. Fold left edge of garment ⅝" over facing and right edge ½" over facing. Stitch neckline. Trim and grade seam.

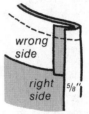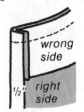

3. Sew zipper in place.

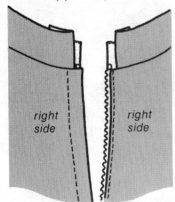

4. Fold tops of zipper to inside and tack in place.

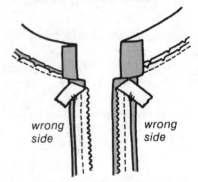

5. Slipstitch facing to zipper tape.

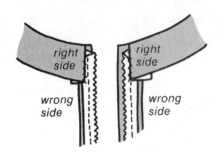

NOTE: For centered zippers, fold both sides of facings back 1" and garment edges ⅝".

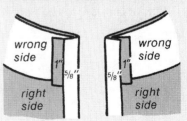

113

Buttons and Buttonholes

With automatic buttonholes a feature on virtually every current sewing machine — even at the lowest price points — there's really no reason to keep sewing pullovers just because you hate to make buttonholes. But if you're still struggling with manual buttonholes on an old machine, sit down and practice as Pati did years ago — one hour or 100 buttonholes, whichever comes first!

No matter what sewing machine you own, you still may wish to experiment with stitch length and width, tension changes, different interfacings or stabilizers, and the "balance" function to achieve "perfect" buttonholes. But remember, in most cases, the button covers up the buttonhole anyway.

Placing Buttonholes

- Horizontal buttonholes should begin ⅛" toward the edge from the center front. Use horizontal buttonholes at points of strain or in close-fitting garments.

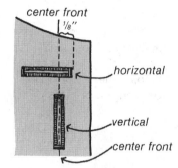

center front
⅛"
horizontal
vertical
center front

- Position vertical buttonholes on the center front line. Use vertical buttonholes in narrow bands or plackets that limit the buttonhole width, or in fabrics with lots of crosswise stretch, like knits.

- Do you suffer from bustline gaposis? Try on the garment — the first button markings should always be at the bust level. Mark all other buttonholes from that point. We usually space them 2-3" apart. It's impossible for pattern companies to mark this position accurately for all figure types.

at bustline

- Buttonholes are on the right-hand side in most women's garments. If you sew the buttonholes in the left side, don't throw away the garment — no one will know. Just say you copied expensive European ready-to-wear — it's all buttoned unisex!

Marking Buttonholes

- Use a marker like the Simflex. It folds up and extends accordian-style. The "windows" at the end of the spokes will allow you to mark horizontal buttonholes and the top ends of vertical buttonholes.

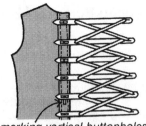

marking vertical buttonholes

- Use a ruler. See-through types are easy to use.

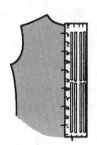

- If you have a buttonhole foot that measures the stitching length as you sew, just mark the point to begin stitching each 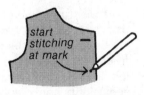 buttonhole. If your machine makes memory buttonholes, make a sample buttonhole on a fabric scrap to test the length. Then your machine can make as many duplicates as you want.

start stitching at mark

- Use your machine buttonhole foot for easy placement. On some machines, you can align the back of the foot with the seam edge for each buttonhole. Stitch in the same direction for each buttonhole.

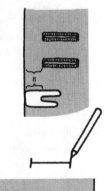

- Mark with a water-soluble or air-erasable marking pen. Test on your fabric first to make sure the marks do come out.

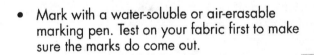

- Scotch™ brand Magic™ Tape — mark the buttonhole length on the tape.

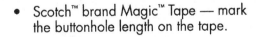

HINT: Use Perfect Sew® to stabilize buttonholes in washable fabrics. It prevents puckering.

Sewing Buttonholes

- Use good-quality thread that is the right size. We like finer threads for lightweight fabrics — lingerie and silk both work.

- Start with a new needle. Have you ever noticed how many button-holes have snag lines extending from the buttonhole stitching? You can prevent it with a new needle that is the right size.

- Adjust the machine tension to make a "pretty" satin stitch on top. Loosen the upper tension or tighten lower tension slightly so the needle and bobbin threads "knot" on the underside. Experiment with different stitch lengths and widths, if necessary.

- Try "taut sewing" when stitching. Hold the fabric taut between your forefingers on either side of the buttonhole while stitching.

Cutting Buttonholes

1. Carefully run a line of seam sealant such as Fray Check™ or Fray No-More between the buttonhole stitching lines. Allow to dry. To control amount, first dip a pin into the liquid and run pin along center of buttonhole.

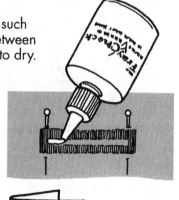

2. Place pins through the ends of the buttonholes. These pins will prevent cutting through the stitching when cutting the buttonhole open.

3. Clip open by folding in half and clipping with embroidery scissors.

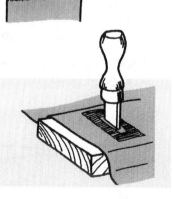

NOTE: Try a buttonhole "cutter" and wooden cutting block. Or, use buttonhole cutter on a rotary mat.

Corded Buttonholes

Buttonholes in knits or other stretchy fabrics can be stabilized by cording them. Cording is also attractive on jackets to give a raised buttonhole look rather than one that sinks into the fabric.

1. If your buttonhole foot doesn't have a hook on the back for cording, insert a pin in the right side of the fabric aligning it with the center line of the buttonhole.

2. Cut an 8-12" length of buttonhole twist. Hook it around the pin or around the buttonhole foot hook.

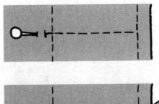

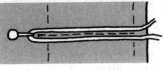

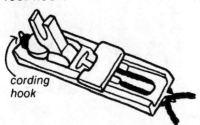

cording hook

NOTE: For a lighter buttonhole, a few strands of regular sewing thread twisted together can be used instead of buttonhole twist. Many sewing machine manuals show how to twist thread together using the bobbin winder.

3. Hold the cord or thread(s) taut while stitching the buttonhole. Stitch over, but not through the cord. Finish the buttonhole.

4. Pull the ends of the cord until the loop disappears under the stitching. Thread a needle with the cord ends and draw to the back. Cut off close to stitching.

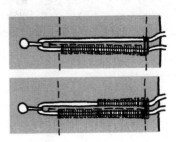

draw up cord

Sew Your Buttons On By Machine! We Do!

They will be much stronger! Use the following instructions for "sew-through" buttons on zigzag machines only:

1. Tape button to fabric with Scotch™ brand Magic™ Tape or glue in place with a dab of water-soluble glue stick.

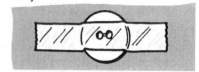

2. Place the button foot on your machine or use the fringe or tailor tack foot if you have them. The high center bar of the foot will create the button's shank.

3. Drop feed dogs on machine or turn to "0" stitch length.

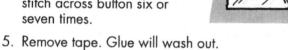

4. Set the stitch width by the holes in the button and stitch across button six or seven times.

5. Remove tape. Glue will wash out.

6. A dab of seam sealant on the thread will strengthen it.

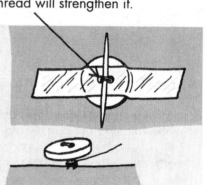

NOTE: For heavier fabrics needing a "shank," use the "feet" mentioned above or sew over a toothpick. Then remove the tape and toothpick, pull the thread tail under the button and wrap it around other threads and tie. This forms the shank.

A Fast Way to Sew Buttons On By Hand

Use a large needle and **four strands of thread** instead of two.

Fold back the edge of the fabric and sew through the fold. The farther away the button, the longer the shank will be.

Then wrap thread around the stitching to form a shank as shown above in the "note."

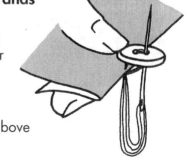

Pockets

In our tailoring book we cover lined pockets and in our pant book we cover trouser pockets. In this book, we give you our favorite additional tips that make pockets totally "painless."

1. Whenever possible, cut pockets on. This works best in full skirts out of lightweight fabrics in solid colors. Check to make sure prints don't show through to outside.

pattern — fabric

Overlap seamlines of pocket and skirt, then cut.

2. When using a lining fabric for pockets, use polyester, as it is strongest. Use a lightweight woven fabric for knits to avoid bulk.

3. Miter square corners as follows:

| Press seam allowances in. | Unfold and trim corner 1/4" from where creases cross. | Fold up 1/4" seam allowance as shown. | Fold seam allowances along creases. |

4. For smooth, round corners on a patch pocket, baste around the pocekt at 1/2". Pull up basting at curves until they are rounded. Press flat. Or, press over a metal pocket template.

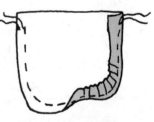

5. To apply any patch pocket quickly, use the "steam baste" method.

Place a 1/4" strip of fusible web under pocket edge. Slightly fuse pocket to garment to by pressing 3-4 seconds. Now the pocket won't slip while topstitching!

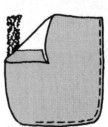

Designing to Individualize

Even though we have both taken pattern-drafting courses, we'd rather use commercial patterns. They are much faster! However, those courses did give us the confidence to personalize a design by making minor changes to patterns. We've selected the eight designing tips we most often use.

Adding Seams

You may want a seam where there isn't one!

Add a center back seam to a jacket for a flattering vertical line.

OR, add seams if you decide to color splice a simple top. Divide the pattern into sections and add seam allowances.

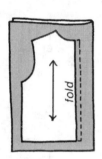

Pattern   **Finished top**

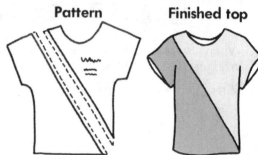

Eliminating Seams

Sometimes pattern companies add a seam only because in the larger sizes they can't get a piece out of a width of fabric. However, there are times you will want to eliminate a seam for speed. If the seam is curved, place the top and bottom of the seam line on the fold. The waistline in our example will be fuller, but you could dart it if you want.

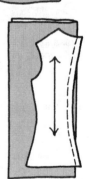

Converting Darts to Tucks or Gathers

Tucks and gathers in pants and skirts are more flattering than darts for many figures, because the soft fullness camouflages lumps and bumps.

½" dart

½" tuck

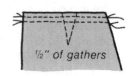

½" of gathers

Changing Grainline in a Skirt

Grainline in a full skirt can be changed to create the effect you want. The most fullness lands where there is bias. The fabric will fall in soft beautiful folds.

This is the most common and universally flattering drape. The fullness is evenly distributed.

Most of the fullness falls at the side seams...If the fabric is stiff, this could make you look wider. (The center front can be cut on the fold.)

Most of the fullness is at the center front — an unusual design effect.

Skirts

Pattern pieces

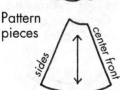

Combining Pattern Pieces

You can combine pattern pieces from different patterns. However, some pieces are easier to interchange than others. It's simple to exchange tops and bottoms in dresses with waist seams and similar shaped sleeves.

At times we have loved a blouse, but felt a gathered sleeve would not fit well under a jacket and wanted a more tailored look. So we find a tailored sleeve to replace the full one. However, the armhole shape from the tailored pattern must be used as well.

You want sleeve "A". . . in blouse "B"

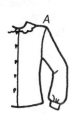 

Overlay the two patterns and trace armhole "A" onto bodice "B." Now sleeve "A" will fit into blouse "B."

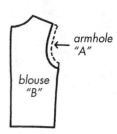

Moving Darts

It's like magic. Practice on old patterns. Bust darts stop 1" from **apex** (point of bust). To move darts, extend the dart lines to the apex.

Original dart.

Extend dart to apex.

Cut out dart. For armhole dart or Princess seam, draw new line into armhole.

Cut and tip pattern piece. Tape old dart closed.

To create an armhole dart add paper behind pattern and redraw dart to within 1" of apex.

To create Princess seam draw line down from apex. Cut apart and add seam allowances. Voila!

 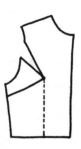 

Add a Yoke

Move the dart to the yoke seam, then ignore it! Just gather the bodice into the yoke instead of darting.

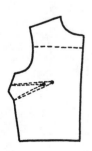  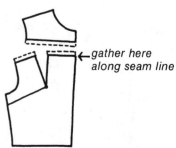

←gather here along seam line

Adding Fullness

Turn a straight skirt into an A-line.

Make a gathered waistline.

Create a dirndl.

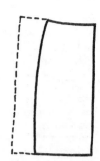

Turn a fitted sleeve into a straight sleeve.

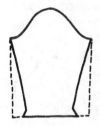

Turn a straight sleeve into a full sleeve. Cut and spread to add fullness throughout.

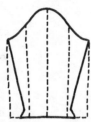

Changing Necklines

A great tip from our book *Sew A Beautiful Wedding* is to cut the bodice front out of featherweight Pellon® interfacing.

- Draw the new neckline shapes on it. Cut away one at a time and hold the bodice front up to you until you decide which you like best.

- To make a facing for the new neckline shape, draw a line 2" from edge of neckline. Add seam allowances to neckline and to facing.

Index

125

TGIF — Thank Goodness It's Finished!